FROM ABERDEEN TO OTTAWA IN 1845

1 ABERDEEN HARBOUR in the 1840s, from which Muir set forth on his Canadian adventure on 3 August 1845 on board the *Lord Seaton*

FROM ABERDEEN TO OTTAWA IN 1845

the Diary of Alexander Muir

edited by
GEORGE A. MACKENZIE

ABERDEEN UNIVERSITY PRESS
Member of Maxwell Macmillan Pergamon Publishing Corporation

First published 1990
Aberdeen University Press

© George A. MacKenzie 1990

British Library Cataloguing in Publication Data

Muir, Alexander
    From Aberdeen to Ottawa in 1845: the diary of Alexander Muir.
    1. Canada. Description & travel, 1841–1864
    I. Title   II. MacKenzie, George A.
    917.10442

ISBN 0 08 037983 4

Typeset from author generated discs
and printed by AUP Glasgow/Aberdeen—a member of BPCC Ltd

CONTENTS

ILLUSTRATIONS

MAPS

FOREWORD

The Centre for Scottish Studies is delighted to add the diary of Alexander Muir to the occasional series published by Aberdeen University Press and sponsored by the Centre. The diary is a fascinating document both through the picture that emerges of its amiable and inquisitive author, and through his account of the incidents and pastimes of an ocean crossing under sail and of travel and life in mid nineteenth-century Canada. In addition, the patient researches of the diary's editor, Mr George MacKenzie, in numerous archives and out of the way sources, have supplied an extra dimension, amounting to a running commentary on incidents, places and people: virtually everyone mentioned in the diary, no matter how obscure, has been tracked down, building up a remarkable picture of the author and his friends, relatives and acquaintances, of the networks of relationships, family or commercial, which connected Scots in Canada to their kinsmen back in Scotland. Finally, to provide background information as to the stage of development Canada had reached at the time of Muir's visit, my colleague Rosemary Tyzack has kindly contributed a brief account of 'Canada in 1845'.

DAVID STEVENSON
Director
Centre for Scottish Studies
University of Aberdeen

PREFACE

Alexander Muir's diary was purchased along with books at a sale in Aberdeen sometime before World War I. It descended to the daughter-in-law of the purchaser, Mrs Sylvia Connon, Cults, Aberdeenshire, and she published a short summary of its contents in 1982: 'Emigrants on the Ottawa', *Aberdeen and North East Scotland Family History Society Newsletter*, no.7 (April 1982), 13–15.

A few months before this I had seen a note in the *Canadian Historical Review*, lxii (1981), 260, announcing that the manuscript had been acquired by the Archives of Ontario. Having taken an interest for ten years or so in emigration from Aberdeen to British North America, and particularly to Ontario, in 1830–45, I wrote to the Ontario Archives, and they supplied me with a photocopy of it. The end result is the annotated transcript of the diary which follows.

I would like to thank the staff of the many archives, museums and societies in both Scotland and Canada from which I have sought information in my research for the notes on the diary and the life of Alexander Muir, and also the following individuals:

Mrs M. Downie, East Kilbride; James Barclay, Islington, Ont.; William R. Clerihue, West Vancouver, BC; Mrs Venetia Crawford, Campbell's Bay, PQ; Dr Bruce S. Elliott, Ottawa, Ont.; Mrs M.N. Gallagher, Cambridge, Ont.; Professor Malcolm A. Gullen, Gloucester, Ont.; John Henry, Agincourt, Ont.; Mrs F. Kimpton, Windermere, BC; Pierre-Louis Lapointe, Hull, PQ; Mrs Joan McKay, Ottawa, Ont.; Miss Ruth McKenzie, Ottawa, Ont.; Eric W. Morse, Wakefield, PQ; William Ramp, Peterborough, Ont.; Mrs Mabel Ringereide, Carleton Place, Ont.; the Misses Elizabeth and Isobel Muir Russell,

Ottawa, Ont.; James Tytler, Hamilton, Ont.; Mrs Doris
Wardlow, Carthage, Missouri; Mrs Lillie J. Barnaby,
Guelph, Ont.; Mrs Ellen Oakes, Elora, Ont.; James H.
Lambert, *Dictionnaire Biographique du Canada*, Toronto; Mrs
Shirley E. Lancaster, Thornhill, Ont.; Mr and Mrs J.R.
Shand, Port Dover, Ont.

Mr J.H.W. Baillie kindly drafted the maps, which were then
redrawn in the Department of Geography, University of Aberdeen. Plate 1 is taken from Aberdeen University Library's copy
of W.H. Bartlett and W.M. Beattie, *Ports, Harbours, Watering
Places and Coast Scenery of Great Britain* (2 vols., London, 1842).
Plate 2 is taken from a drawing in the same library, Department
of Manuscripts, MS 2769/1/25/5. All the remaining plates are
from the Glasgow University Library copy of W.H. Bartlett,
Canadian Scenery Illustrated (2 vols., London, 1842).

Finally, I am most grateful to the Archives of Ontario for
permission to publish this transcript of the Diary, and to the
Centre for Scottish Studies, University of Aberdeen, for the
work undertaken there in preparing this work for publication.

GEORGE A. MACKENZIE

INTRODUCTION

i Alexander Muir

In 1845 a middle-aged Aberdeen lawyer, Alexander Muir, set off to visit Canada. He was not emigrating or travelling on business, but went for family reasons and simply for fun. He had a brother and a sister who had emigrated to Canada, and he wanted to see them. But it is also likely that their letters, and the stories he had heard in Aberdeen from the many men from the region who had been to Canada to trade or for other reasons, had roused his curiosity about the country. By 1845 Muir was a sober and respected figure in Aberdeen's prosperous middle class, well known in professional and commercial circles, who had bought a modest country estate and thus established himself as a landed gentleman. But after a quiet career of professional diligence he felt the need for a little adventure, an urge to break out and experience an ocean crossing under sail and a vast country already boasting thriving cities, but in which the untamed wilderness was never far away.

Before he sailed from Aberdeen, Alexander promised his young son George to write to him describing his experiences. The result was the letter-diary printed below, beginning on 3 August 1845 when his ship sailed from Aberdeen and ending (at least in the surviving manuscript) on 11 October the same year— in a canoe far up the Ottawa River! All that is known of his travels thereafter is contained in a few notes he made in the diary about letters he posted at later dates, and in a letter (printed in Appendix 1) which he wrote while in Canada to his brother-in-law. On 18 October he was in Kingston, at the head of the St Lawrence as it flows out of Lake Ontario. By 20 November he was in Port Dover on Lake Erie, in south Ontario, writing to his son about 'my journey, Indians, etc., and that I thought I would winter in the States'. Three days later he was in Brampton, sixteen miles west of Toronto, and while he was in that area he doubtless fulfilled his intention to visit his brother George, whose family was settled five miles from Elora, which itself lies fourteen miles north west of Guelph. Presumably he then moved on into the States, making for new York and returning to Aberdeen from there. It seems likely that originally his diary continued to describe his adventures long after the point at which it now ends, and it is to be hoped that this lost section will be located one day.

Who was Alexander Muir? His parents, George Muir and Mary Gray (who could claim a distant family connection with Lord Gray) were married in the parish of Slains, Aberdeenshire, on 2 April 1781. George was tenant of the farm of Netherleask in the same parish, and there Alexander was born on 23 November 1793, the sixth child (and third and last son) of a family of eight. Both his elder brothers, George and John, became farmers, but Alexander attended Aberdeen Grammar School (1807–8) and Marischal College, Aberdeen (1809–13), though (as was common at the time) he left the latter without a degree. He then served a legal apprenticeship with Thomas Sangster, and was admitted to the Society of Advocates in Aberdeen in 1817. Muir's career thereafter is perhaps best described as solid and worthy rather than distinguished. His work was mainly of a routine nature—acting for clients in the buying, selling and leasing of property in the area, and in the winding up of the estates of the deceased. His education suggests that his father was prospering, and Alexander himself clearly made a good living from the law. As early as 1825 he was involved in the foundation of the Aberdeen Town and Country Bank, becoming a shareholder. On 11 August 1831 Muir married Mary Ann Catherine Kilgour, the daughter of Patrick Kilgour of Woodside. Alexander Muir had acted as one of the executors of Patrick's will after his death the previous year, and it was doubtless this that brought him into contact with his future wife.

The marriage was probably financially advantageous, for in 1835 Muir was able to acquire the lands of South Loirston and part of the town and lands of Cove. This property lay south of the River Dee in Kincardineshire, opposite Aberdeen, and the opening of a suspension bridge across the river in 1832 was leading to fast development in the area; previously the nearest bridge had been that at Bridge of Dee, about two miles upstream. Though remaining resident in Aberdeen itself at first, Muir launched into the fashionable pursuit of agricultural improvement on his new estate with enthusiasm. His wider interest in the affairs of the neighbourhood are reflected in the records of the parish of Nigg, in which South Loirston lay. He can be traced making donations to collections, helping purchase communion cups, and taking an active part in the appointment of a schoolmaster and a minister. His services to the area were recognised in 1840 when his tenants, friends and neighbours organised a complimentary dinner for him in Cove Hotel. He took a particular interest in education, and the chairman at the dinner praised him particularly for being 'of the utmost service in conferring upon the youth of Cove and that district the blessings of moral and religious education, where the utmost ignorance had previously prevailed'.

Public achievement was however accompanied by private sorrow. His wife Mary bore him two sons, Patrick Kilgour Muir (1832–6) and George Falconer Muir (born 1836—and for whom Muir was to compile his travel diary in 1845), but she died on 27 April 1837. It was probably after her death that Muir took up residence at South Loirston, building a modest but substantial mansion, Loirston House, in 1842 at a cost of £800. But by 1845 the wanderlust had seized him, perhaps because he realised that if he was going to see something of the wider world he better do so before he grew much older. In the spring he was advertising Loirston House for letting, and he arranged for his surviving son, George, to be boarded at a private school in Aberdeen, Bellevue Academy. Luggage— including a feather bed!—was packed, and 3 August he set sail on the *Lord Seaton*.

What followed can be left to the diary itself. It shows Muir taking a lively interest in everything about him, fascinated by the characters he meets, involving himself in whatever was going on from setting up a sabbath school for the children on the ship to acting as a judge at an agricultural show in Canada.

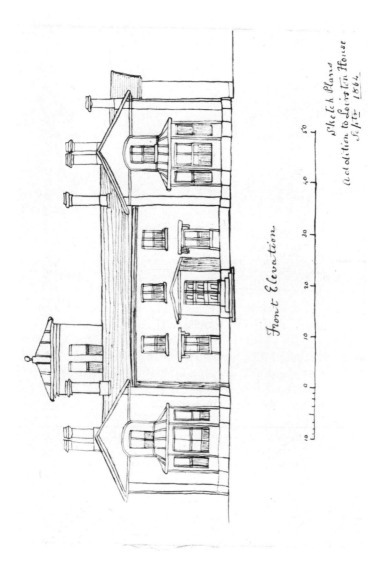

Front Elevation

Sketch Plans
Addition to Loirston House
Septr 1864

2   LOIRSTON HOUSE, the central block of which was built by Alexander Muir in 1842

A diligent tourist, he visited notable buildings in the towns, admired the scenery, fitting in all he could as he bustled around under sail, in steamboats, in carriages and canoes, and on foot. Of a social disposition, the dignified Aberdeen lawyer showed an ability to mix with people from a wide variety of backgrounds—and remarkably often he managed to trace some link between then and acquaintances of his back in Scotland. Altogether he comes over, in the pages of the diary, as an energetic and genial man—though happy to share Canadian dislike of 'Yankees', and treating the spectacle of thriving Roman Catholicism with a sort of horrified fascination: where a modern tourist out for naughty titillation while away from home might visit strip joints, Muir got his kicks for free by visiting nunneries and hearing mass!

Alexander Muir was back in Aberdeen by 4 April 1846, when he attended a meeting of Nigg Parochial Board. Probably he had wintered in the United States, as he had told his son George he intended to, before returning home from an ice-free port there. Soon he was busily involved in local affairs again, taking a leading part in the activities of the parochial board. In 1849 he became the board's chairman, but resigned the following year through ill health. His interest in education continued (in 1846 the heritors of Cove and the kirk session of Nigg met in his offices to appoint a schoolmaster), as did that in agriculture—he joined the Highland and Agricultural Society of Scotland in 1847. A new interest about this time was railways, for the line from the south to Aberdeen was constructed over Muir's lands. But, as before his visit to Canada, the outcome of personal and family affairs was less happy than his involvement in public and professional life. On 28 December 1847 Muir married Jane B. Ferguson, the daughter of a neighbour, James Ferguson of Altens, who like Muir himself was both an advocate and an improving landlord. But his second marriage proved even shorter than his first, for Jane died in January 1849, aged twenty-six. Moreover tragedy struck the family of his younger sister Margaret, which he had got to know on his Canadian journey. The year after he had visited them her husband, Alexander Finlay, and George, her third son, had been drowned, and the family fell on hard times. Alexander sent financial help. On 24 January 1847 he sent £20 to Captain Petrie, an acquaintance made in Canada and obviously trusted, to pay bills for Margaret. Another £10 was sent on 14 July to help pay her late husband's creditors, but problems remained. The family evidently contemplated returning to Scotland, for in a letter of 24 July 1848 sending more money Muir said that though things were bad in Bytown (Ottawa) they were bad in Scotland as well (this was a period of economic depression), so they should stay where they were. On 9 October 1850 Alexander and his brother John each sent £5—and John reported that Alexander was very ill with jaundice.

Alexander Muir died on 13 November 1850: he was buried, as were his two wives and his son Patrick, in Nellfield Cemetery, Aberdeen. His other son George, recipient of the letter diary of his father's Canadian tour, became a writer and moved to Edinburgh, selling Loirston House in 1863. Alexander's will reveals that he also had an illegitimate son, another Alexander, born in 1828. His father left him £220 and tenement property in Aberdeen. The younger Alexander started off his career serving an apprenticeship at sea with an Aberdeen skipper, but subsequently became a vet near Dunbar. In 1877 he killed himself, taking strychnine after the police were called to intervene in a drunken quarrel between him and his wife.

Loirston House stood for a century as a monument to Alexander Muir, lawyer and landowner, before being demolished in the 1970s as a tide of housing submerged the lands he had worked so hard to improve. But now his diary can replace his house by providing a monument to a happy and uncharacteristically adventurous episode in his life.

The diary of Alexander Muir as it exists in the Archives of Ontario is in Muir's own handwriting, and is evidently a fair copy he made of the text of the letters he sent to his son George before posting them. Thus at the end of his entry for 8 September he notes that the letter containing the text up to this point had been posted to his son at Quebec on 10 September; and the beginning of the letter indicates that he had begun to write it on 9 August. The following page in the surviving diary was left blank, and subsequently used to record the posting of

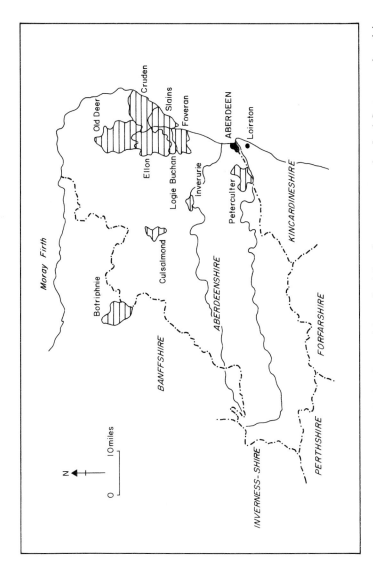

Map 1 North East Scotland, showing parishes of origin of passengers on the *Lord Seaton* mentioned in Alexander Muir's Diary.

later letters. In the transcript of the diary printed below these memoranda have been transferred to the end of the text.

Thereafter it is likely that, as Muir prepared each successive letter for posting, he copied it into the diary version that now survives—though no longer noting where each letter ended in this text, which was to be kept for his own use; several times he calls it his 'log'. There is, however, one puzzling feature of the text. Up to 18 September the year date is correctly given as 1845: but all the subsequent entries give it as 1846. Had Muir been writing up the diary in 1845, immediately after the events it records, it is hard to see how he didn't quickly notice and correct this slip. The most logical explanation is that he was writing up the diary considerably later, in 1846, and by error dated the entries by the current year. It is even possible that he wrote up these later sections of the diary after his return to Aberdeen, having recovered his original letters from his son.

The following conventions have been followed in transcribing the diary. The occasional minor spelling errors (which must have amused the young George Muir—if they were in the version sent to him) have been silently corrected, and some changes to punctuation and capitalisation have been made. The names of ships have been italicised, and the form in which dates are given at the beginning of entries has been standardised and corrected (thus concealing the 1845/1846 confusion). The numbered headings which split the diary into sections have been added by me, but the other headings are Muir's own.

The diary is followed by appendices containing the text of one of Muir's letters written while in Canada, and by transcripts of two short accounts of voyages from Aberdeen to Quebec in the 1830s: these accounts are of special interest in relating the experiences of the less well-off, travelling 'steerage'—a much more crowded and less comfortable experience than that of 'cabin' passengers like Muir.

(Sources for Muir's life and family: T. Watt, *Aberdeen Grammar School, Roll of Pupils, 1795–1919, annotated from 1863*, Aberdeen, 1923; P.J. Anderson, ed., *Fasti Academiae Mariscallanae Aberdonensis, 1593–1860*, ii, *Officers, Graduates and Alumni*, New Spalding Club, 1898; J.A. Henderson, ed., *History of the Society of Advocates, in Aberdeen*, New Spalding Club, 1912; Census records of 1841 and 1851 for the parishes of Slains and St Nicholas

(Aberdeen), Aberdeenshire, and Nigg, Kincardineshire; Old Parochial Registers for parishes of Slains, Cruden and St Nicholas (Aberdeen), Aberdeenshire and Nigg, Kincardineshire; *Scottish Notes and Queries*, July 1893, 28; *Transactions of the Highland and Agricultural Society of Scotland, 1847–51, Membership Lists*; *Prize Essays and Transactions of the Highland and Agricultural Society of Scotland*, xiii, 1841, 163–80; *New Statistical Account*, xi, *Forfar-Kincardine* (Edinburgh, 1845), 200, 205; Muir and the Aberdeen Town and County Bank, see Glasgow University Archives, UGD129/3/2/1; *Kincardineshire Sasines Index, 1781–1850*, no. 351 of 16 March 1835; *1852–3*, no. 259 of 17 November 1852; *1856–1860*, nos. 160, 161, 168; *1861–64*, nos. 79, 81, 258, 362, 406, 412; Will and Inventory of Alexander Muir, advocate, Scottish Record Office [SRO], SC1/37/29, f.470 and SC1/36/29, f.977, Inventory of Mrs Jane Ferguson or Muir, SRO, SC5/41/13, f.476; Will of Miss Jane Muir, SRO, SC1/37/81, f.715; Parish of Nigg, Kincardineshire, Register of Doctrine and Discipline, SRO, CH2/554/3 (1817–1839) and 4 (1839–1862); Minutes Book of the Parochial Board of Nigg, Kincardineshire, 1845–1866, Grampian Regional Archives; Kilgour Papers, MS2769/1/25/1 and 5, Aberdeen University Archives; Information from the Misses E. and I.M. Russell, Ottawa, Ont., Royal College of Veterinary Surgeons, London, and Mrs Findlay, Librarian, University of Glasgow Veterinary Department Library, Bearsden; *Haddingtonshire Register*, 1874–7; *Haddingtonshire Courier*, 19 October 1877; *Aberdeen Journal*, 26 March 1845, 31 January 1849, 20 November 1850, 3 June 1857; *Aberdeen Herald*, 17 June 1835, 27 February 1836, 6 May 1837, 19 October 1839, 4, 11 April, 2 May, 6 June, 28 November 1840, 24 July, 16, 23 and 30 October 1841, 5 February and 12 March 1842, 4 March, 17 June, 22 July 1843, 24 February, 18 May, 10 August 1844).

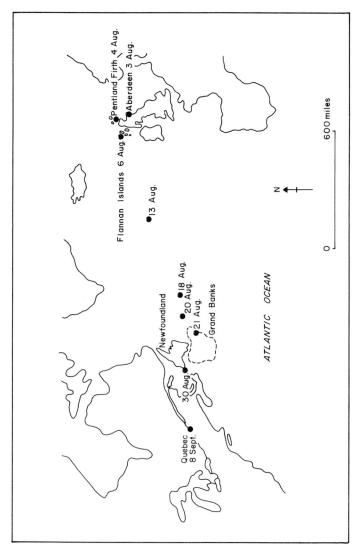

Map 2   The voyage of the *Lord Seaton* from Aberdeen to Quebec, 3 August — 8 September 1845, according to positions given in Muir's Diary.

ii Canada in 1845

Rosemary M. Tyzack

Alexander Muir's visit to the Canadas coincided with a period of crisis and uncertainty in Canadian history. After some fifty years and more of comparatively peaceful economic development and political stability under British rule the Canadian colonies faced rebellion in 1837; a shift in British economic policy away from imperial preference which threatened their staple exports of timber and wheat to Britain; renewed border disputes with the USA in which Britain seemed to be leaning over backwards to appease the Americans; and increased powers of local self-government which pleased Canadian radicals but could also be seen as a sign that Britain was no longer interested in retaining control over the Canadian colonies, and as a prelude to independence.

The British colonies in what is now Canada (the Atlantic provinces of Newfoundland, Prince Edward Island, New Brunswick and Nova Scotia, and the inland provinces of Lower Canada and Upper Canada, after 1841 the united province of Canada East and Canada West) had long been seen as lands of opportunity by the Scots, as by the English, Welsh and Irish. Many Orcadians recruited by the Hudson's Bay Company for the fur trade had stayed on, Scottish soldiers in the Seven Years War had received land grants, and Scottish traders supplying the army in that war turned to organising Canadian trade after peace in 1763, securing the dominant positions they were to maintain through much of the eighteenth and nineteenth centuries. They were joined by many from the Highlands and the Western Isles in the eighteenth century. Predominantly Gaelic speaking, often Roman Catholic, emigrating in family groups, they frequently settled in distinctive highland communities, particularly in Nova Scotia, Upper Canada and Prince Edward Island.

After the Napoleonic wars, with substantial changes in agriculture and growing industrialisation in Britain, emigration to Canada, as to the USA, became a flood. In contrast to earlier emigration, emigrants now represented a cross-section of Scottish society, Lowlanders as well as Highlanders, from the country and from the towns, from business and the professions as well as the working classes. Increasingly they moved into Upper Canada. Muir's relatives on the Ottawa were part of the newest frontier. Emigrants now tended to move as individuals rather than in groups, even though many were encouraged to take the step by letters from relatives and friends already in Canada, and others were helped by government or charitable resettlement schemes. They benefited from the comparatively cheap fares for the transatlantic crossing as boats carrying timber and wheat from Canada were looking for a return freight, and many called in at local Scottish ports, not just at Liverpool and Glasgow, saving the cost of travel in Britain. Many emigrants were attracted by cheap land and by opportunities for investment, but they were also attracted by a more classless society, by greater religious freedom and by more extensive political rights than in Britain.

The Canadian economy was based on exports of furs, fish, timber and (by the 1830s) wheat and flour to a growing British market, fostered by British preferential duties, by the needs of an expanding Canadian population, and by exploitation of the St Lawrence river and the Great lakes as a trade route for American as well as Canadian produce. By the 1840s the fur trade was concentrated in the hands of the Hudson's Bay Company, the North West Company having been bought out in 1821. The Canadian timber industry gained from Britain's need to import timber during the French Revolutionary and Napoleonic wars when Baltic supplies were cut off and then from the growing British demand for timber for the construction industry, aided by British preferential duties after 1809. While much timber cutting on the St Lawrence area was tied in with clearing land for agriculture and was often undertaken by the farmers themselves on the Ottawa, it was also big business, specialist firms employing lumber jacks, organising transport and developing mills for sawn timber. The timber industry offered a source of supplementary income for farmers starting up, or high wages for lumber jacks, attracting single young male emigrants, while the lumber camps offered a market for farm produce. The timber trade also provided investment opportunities attracting Scots. Many Scots were also involved in pioneer farming, encouraged by cheap land. The Governments in Upper Canada and in the Atlantic Provinces at first gave virtually free grants of land, but from the 1820s the settler had to purchase land either from the government or from big land companies like the Canada Land Company in Upper Canada or the British-American Land Company in Lower Canada. Some just settled on new land without acquiring a legal title to it. While many farmers used primitive techniques to clear the bush, more sophisticated techniques and machinery were being adopted in longer settled areas. New opportunities for settlers were also opening up in milling, often combined with store-keeping, though increasingly the wheat trade was being organised by exporting firms in Montreal. Both the wheat and timber trades were helped enormously by the improvements in Canadian waterways, often financed by the British government, which looked to waterways for the transport of British troops and the protection of the border with the USA.

Canadian society was more open than in Britain. There was no hereditary aristocracy, and, while the Church of England had been initially given special privileges, neither it nor the Church of Scotland held the dominant positions they had in Britain. Many Canadians would criticise the power and influence of the great land speculators, the Montreal traders, and government officials, or the pretensions of the Church of England and of the Church of Scotland, but the chance to get on in Canada depended on skills and wealth rather than on birth or religious affiliation. In recognising the French Canadians' church, law, education and language in the Quebec Act (1774) Britain gave the Roman Catholic church greater recognition and Roman Catholics more rights than in contemporary Britain, and many Roman Catholic Highlanders benefited from this. The Roman Catholic Church established bishoprics throughout Canada, and provided much of the education and welfare in Lower Canada. Roman Catholics were not barred from voting or from holding public office. The Church of England and the Church of Scotland were given financial aid by the governments towards clerical stipends and church building, but the efforts of some Anglicans and some Presbyterians to ensure that their churches became fully established were defeated, and in particular the Anglican church in Upper Canada never gained the control over education it would have liked. The Methodist and Baptist churches, often linked to the American churches, and the Free Church of Scotland, gained increasing numbers and respect. Provision for education in Canada had initially been rather uneven but by the mid nineteenth century the colonies had developed systems which were at least on a par with British provision. Lower Canada, following the Lower Canada School Acts of 1845 and 1846, had a dual state aided system of Roman Catholic and of Protestant schools managed by local elected school commissioners, topped by 'colleges classiques' in the French tradition of classical humanistic learning. McGill University, modelled on the lines of the non-sectarian privately endowed universities of America and after 1852 Laval University, modelled on French Catholic universities, provided education and training in the law, medicine, science and the arts and theology. Upper Canada in contrast developed a non-sectarian public school system, also state aided and managed by locally elected school trustees and annual district meetings. Separate schools based on religious denomination were however allowed. Students could then go on to denominational institutions like Queen's at Kingston founded by the Presbyterians. The state endowed secular University of Toronto was to be established in 1849. The Atlantic provinces were similarly building up their schools and colleges.

Scots contributed much to the development of the churches and of educational institutions in Canada. The first Roman Catholic bishop of Upper Canada, Alexander Macdonell, came from Glengarry; the first Anglican bishop of Upper Canada, John Strachan, from Aberdeen; and the second Anglican bishop in Lower Canada, Charles Stewart, from Galloway. Scots had considerable influence not only in extending the work of the churches but also in shaping their policies—for instance, the more popular element in church government introduced to the

Anglican church by Bishop Strachan. Scots were the mainstay of the Presbyterian churches in Canada, supported by organisations in Scotland like the 'Glasgow Colonial Society'. Similarly many Scots helped to staff and to shape the educational systems. They contributed to the demand that education should be available for all but also that the 'lad o' pairts' should be able to make his way up the educational ladder, and in the universities to the tradition of combining humanistic and vocational training.

The Canadian colonies had benefited greatly from their connections with Britain in the late eighteenth and early nineteenth centuries, from British protected markets for their staples of furs, timber and wheat; from the inflow of British people and British investment; and from British diplomatic and military protection from their neighbour, the USA. Britain had favoured the colonies as sources of timber and grain which were important for her security as well as economy, and as havens for her 'surplus' population and for the Loyalists leaving the USA after the American Revolution. But the 1830s and 1840s saw the imperial connection being questioned both in Canada and in Britain, and latent social and political pressures in the Canadian colonies coming to the fore. The colonies had a measure of internal self-government, through their own local legislatures, with easy qualifications for becoming members of the elected assemblies and for voting. Many Canadians, British and French, however, were demanding further control over their own affairs. Many radicals and many farmers were critical of the political influence of land speculators, government officials and traders whom they considered were unduly supported by the British government and its local representatives, the British governors. They were looking for popular control over government, in particular the right to appoint members of the Executive Council—a right which Britain still retained. Many radicals were in contact with British Radical MPs such as Joseph Hume, MP successively for Aberdeen, Middlesex and Montrose, or with leaders of movements for broadening the franchise like the Chartists. Others looked towards what they considered to be the more liberal constitution of the USA. While most radicals and reformers wanted to employ only peaceful methods of persuasion, extremists rebelled both in Upper and

Lower Canada in 1837. In Upper Canada the rebellion was led by a Scot, William Lyon Mackenzie from Dundee, and in Lower Canada by the French Canadian Louis Papineau. While some historians see the roots of nationalism and a growing wish for complete independence in these upheavals, others argue that Canadians merely wanted more local self-government while still maintaining the British connection. Britain's policies seemed to pose a threat to this connection—phasing out imperial preference (most notably with the lowering of the preferential duties on timber in 1842 and the abolition of the protective corn laws in 1846); cutting back on its military commitment to the Canadas; making boundary settlements with USA in 1842 and 1846 which seemed to give away chunks of territory which many Canadians felt they had at least as good a claim to as the USA; and her concession of the right of Canadians to choose whom should form their government. All this led many to conclude, then and later, that Britain was preparing to sever her connection with the colonies. With hindsight historians would now argue that Britain was feeling her way to a new political accommodation with the colonies, increasingly confident that greater political freedom, strengthening trade links founded in British and Canadian economic expansion, and shared cultural traditions would consolidate British-Canadian ties, underpinned as they also were by the networks of family connections which Alexander Muir so clearly depicts.

BIBLIOGRAPHY

Kenneth McNaught's *The Penguin History of Canada* (London, 1988 edition) is a good, widely available, account of Canada's history. J.M. Bumstead in his pamphlet *The Scots in Canada* (Ottawa, Canadian Historical Association, 1982) gives a succinct overview of the role of the Scots in Canadian development, while W. Stanford Reid (ed.), *The Scottish tradition in Canada* (Toronto, 1976) provides more extensive accounts of the Scots contribution to Canadian settlement, economy, politics, the army, and culture and religion. J.M. Bumstead has also looked at emigration to Canada in *The Peoples' Clearance: Highland Emigration to British North America 1775–1815* (Edinburgh, 1982), as has Marjory Harper in her work on emigration from North East Scotland, *Emigration from North East Scotland*, volume i, *Willing exiles*; volume ii, *Beyond the broad Atlantic* (Aberdeen, 1988). R.C. Harris and J. Warkentin describe the progress of Canadian settlement in *Canada before Confederation: a study in historical geography* (London, 1975). More comprehensive coverage of Canada's history is provided in the Canadian Centenary Series, published by McClelland and Stewart and Oxford University Press, particularly G.M. Craig *Upper Canada. The formative years, 1784–1841* (Toronto, 1963), J.M.S. Careless, *The Union of the Canadas 1841–1857* (Toronto and London, 1968) and W.S. MacNutt, *The Atlantic provinces. The emergence of colonial society 1712–1857* (Toronto and London, 1961).

THE DIARY OF ALEXANDER MUIR

1 THE VOYAGE

Saturday 9 August 1845. On board the *Lord Seaton*,[1] 'outward bound' for Quebec. My Dear Geordy,[2]
It is only eight days since we bade adieu! at the *Seaton's* side, with hearts full of emotion and hope soon to meet again. But that little barque has already imperceptibly glided me 800 miles[3] across the mighty deep. No doubt many a time have you been asking 'How far will papa be yet'? You know, I promised not to forget you, and to give you some account of what was daily passing around me, however trifling—You promising to give me a similar account of your progress at school or elsewhere. And to begin at the beginning.

Sunday 3 August 1845. Sailed this morning as you know and will no doubt long remember with 71 souls on board; of these 64 are passengers—17 male, 13 female adults and 34 children from 4 months to 14 years of age.[4] Only myself and a Mr James Gordon,[5] a commission agent, in the cabin. All more or less sick. I was able to be at dinner.[6] The wind fair all day, made a good run.

Monday 4 August. Wind continues fair. Passed through the Pentland Firth[7] this morning—sick today, not able to rise, but not so sick as to get a 'clearance'.

Tuesday 5 August. Off the Sutherland coast. Wind ahead. Kept company with, and spoke the *Prince George* of Alloa bound for Quebec. This vessel is nearly 60 years of age![8]

Wednesday 6 August. Fair wind off the Lewis Isles. The Flannel Islands[9] in view today, the last land to be seen, and for three weeks we bid mother earth adieu! There is something in this, which casts a gloom over the mind from the great uncertainty of reaching another shore in safety.

Thursday 7 August. Wind fair. Pleasant day. Sickness disappeared. I have been only one day absent from dinner. All the steerage passengers ordered on deck by the captain and names called over, in search of 'strayed sheep'.[10] Number of whales playing around us, sometimes diving beneath the vessel and coming up at the other side. Could have leaped from the ship upon their backs. Some of the passengers proposed shooting at them but the great leviathans of the deep sheered off upon the first intelligence of this bloody intention, at the same time they contemptuously exhibited to us our feeble efforts to injure them, as they disappeared.

Friday 8 August. Light breeze—pleasant weather and fair wind. The passengers are now all free from sickness and they begin to display their varied characters. They appear to be rather a respectable and *comfortable* class of people, such, I would say from what I have learned, as will do well in America. We have one old eccentric character amongst us. He says he is going out to see a son. He tells a number of amusing stories. He is from Middle Third, Parish of Botriphny.[11] He goes by the name of 'Old Johnthan'. He is upwards of 70 years of age, has not a tooth in his head. He says he gave one to the minister, and one to each elder, and told them that as he had brought none into the parish he should take none out of it. The passengers and sailors enjoyed themselves this evening with a trip upon the light fantastic toe. Mr Allardyce from Cruden[12] playing the violin, I accompanying him with the tambarine. One of the sailors (Lucas) danced Jacky Tar[13] in perfect character.

Saturday 9 August. Fresh breeze all last night. Wind going rather ahead, and looks a little stormy but still at 8 knots an hour. Had a glass of brandy and water with the captain and drank the usual 'Saturday night at sea' toasts.

Sunday 10 August. The wind continues fair but light. Nearly one third of our way to the Banks of Newfoundland. The captain intimated to the passengers that there would be public worship at 12 o'clock. Consequently at that hour all convened, young and old, master and crew, excepting the helmsman, around the 'capstan' (the reading desk). The day was beautiful, and the muster of so many human beings all arranged upon the deck of a small barque in the midst of the Mighty Ocean for such a purpose was truly interesting and pleasing. The services were conducted by a Mr Logan, an episcopal schoolmaster from the parish of Cruden.[14] The psalmody by a Free Church precentor![15] Although we have a variety of sects on board all seemed to merge their sectarian differences into *the* one Grand Focus! As I mentioned we have 31 children[16] on board and in some measure to pass the time as profitably as possible I intimated that I would open a Sabbath evening school after dinner. This was eagerly listened to. Behold me sitting upon deck with about 20 boys and girls around me, going through all the religious exercises of Sabbath teaching. Many of the children are excellent scholars. One girl, who rather excelled, on being asked who had taught her, answered, Mr Middleton, minister of Culsamond![17] The little things as well as their mothers are delighted with the idea of a Sabbath School on board ship and with the notice taken of them.

I think a Sabbath may be better spent upon the sea than at land. The very idea of being 1500 miles from any land raises the mind to a feeling of adoration, far above what it can be raised upon land. There is nothing here to interrupt the serenity of the thoughts. Let us come tonight, and behold the last streak of twilight, reaching along the horizon, and throwing an instinctive light upon the face of the great waters, gradually passing away as you steadily look over the ship's side—and reflecting upon the boundlessness and unknown deep of the sea around you, gives one a feeling of loneliness, of dread and I may say a melancholy foreboding which nothing else in *nature* can give, and which nothing in *nature* can take away. The mind centres in *one* resting place for relief, and every night as yet has been followed by a cheerful morning, and the last week has closed and the present begun with the most pleasant reflection of the Almighty's goodness towards us.

Monday 11 August. Again delighted on stepping out this morning from my berth, and seeing all cheerful and gay, with fresh breeze and all sails set. You would be delighted with this voyage, My Dear Geordy.

Tuesday 12 August. Still a fresh breeze from the right quarter, 'twixt 8 and 9 knots. A schooner hove in sight with signals of distress, caused considerable excitement on board. Bore down upon her. Found her to be a Guernsey ship from Newfoundland. Had been out 34 days! Had lost her longitude. The master must have been a Johny Raw of a skipper. I am now quite at home in the vessel. Our captain is a very excellent, steady man and we spend our time very pleasantly together. In the evenings we take a single glass of brandy toddy, sing a song. My shipmate Mr Gordon sings very nice. We sometimes invite a steerage passenger to take a glass with us by way of enlivening the evening. Some very respectable men amongst them, as also intelligent. Several have been at America before, from whom we hear many strange things. This evening a great number of 'puffy dunders'[18] have been playing round and round our vessel to the great amusement of the passengers. The sailors don't like them. They say it is the sign of bad weather. We shall mark.

Wednesday 13 August. Wind right astern. Heavy swell causing the ship to roll mightily. All well.

Thursday 14 August. Wind as yesterday. Have run upwards of 150 miles last 24 hours. The rolling of the vessel has caused me to pitch up my dinner! The only remark worthy of being recorded today.

Friday 15 August. The wind unchanged. A remarkable cirumstance—the length of time this wind has continued so near the same point, to us favourable. The sea very smooth. To kill time Mr Gordon and I amused ourselves issuing theatrical bills intimating certain amusements which were to take place in the evening. The performers being the passengers and sailors named in the bill. A dance and singing accordingly took place. The music as usual.

Saturday 16 August. Light breezes but fair. Very warm. Thermometer at 70°. A concert proposed and agreed to by the captain. (But no dancing, being Saturday night). Bills stuck upon the mainmast intimating the same, giving the names of the various performers. This created a good deal of fun but none refused to sing. Seats were arranged on deck for the performance and upwards of 20 excellent songs were sung. An appropriate air was played 'twixt each song by our instrumental band. The sailors joined in the performance. The shark and several of the finny tribe popped up and seemed to listen with amazement to the unusual strains during the concert. It is rather curious that, altho' so far from land, we daily see birds. For the last two or three nights the same kind of bird which I observed about Loirston last winter is constantly fluttering about us. I find they are from Newfoundland. The sailors call them the 'Mother Carey Bird' from their carry[ing] their young. The 'storm petrel' is their proper name. It is clear they must have come from the Banks of Newfoundland to us a distance of 2000 miles!!

Sunday 17 August. Very little wind. Thermometer 72° in cabin. All on board dressed. Upon deck the day is lovely, the sky without a cloud. The atmosphere dry and comfortably warm. The sea as if oil had been poured upon its bosom. The ship imperceptibly moving at the rate of about two knots—the passengers walking about in a reflective mood, as if viewing their own tinted fields. In short, when I stepped from my cabin and beheld all these, nature seemed watching in breathless silent anxiety, ready to burst forth with acclamation of praise at the approach of its great maker. In the midst of this serenity and calmness young and old assembled at twelve o'clock on deck for public worship, which was conducted as last Sabbath and listened to with equal interest. After dinner my little school assembled on deck, children most diligent and attentive—all had their tasks and prizes were distributed. This day closes the second week of my nautical life. The time has passed pleasantly, but think, my dear little fellow, in this short space of fourteen days I have been carried 2,000 miles from you! Nearly two thirds of my journey by water. Goodnight.

Monday 18 August. The weather continues the same. Thermometer 71°. This day's amusement is to be walking matches—

round the deck. Thirty-five rounds is a mile.[19] Wrote the following upon a slip of paper, sealed it up in a bottle and threw it overboard. 'Latitude 48° 24', longitude 43°. The barque *Lord Seaton* of Aberdeen, Captain Talbot, from Aberdeen to Quebec with 64 passengers. All well. Should this be found at a considerable distance please make it public. Alex Muir, James Gordon cabin passengers'.[20]

Tuesday 19 August. The wind rather too much to the windward, but a beautiful day. Thermometer 69° in the cabin. The temperature of the sea 62°. The air and sea keep nearly the same temperature in this latitude (48° 5) (This is the case in all latitudes where soundings cannot be made). Passed upward of forty vessels homeward bound. Spoke one four weeks out from Quebec. We have been only 16 days and sailed double the distance. The dolphin has followed us most of the day. It is a most beautiful looking fish in the water. We tried to catch them, but they would not hook. The captain fired a gun several times at them as they approached the surface, but did no execution. Saw a whale or some other large animal floating on the surface of the water apparently dead. In the afternoon we were surrounded with *shoals of herring*. The dolphins came in contact with them, when a most lively chase took place. They pursued, the herrings running out of the water something in the same manner as I have seen water birds half run, half fly on the surface of the water. The herrings at first pushed desperately for their lives, but being out of their element could not long continue, consequently the dolphins overtook them and feasted copiously.

Wednesday 20 August. Fine clear morning but headwind six points out of course. Took in the main royals for first time. A large ice berg in view, two very high points on it, one apparently as high as the topmast of our ship, the other somewhat lower. Several more ice bergs have come in view, one appeared at first in the shape of a sugar loaf and as large as the new markets of Aberdeen.[21] As we approached them they assumed various shapes. The last was the largest of all; it appeared to be as large as the castle of Edinburgh. The captain says he never saw any of greater size. We supposed it to be nearly 300 feet above the water. It is said two thirds remain below the water! It is rare to see them in so southern a latitude at this season of the year, latitude 48° 10′ longitude 48°. Thick and foggy pm.

Banks of Newfoundland

Thursday 21 August. Calm—very warm. Thermometer 70°. *Sounded* for the first time, in 50 fathoms of water, knew thereby that we had reached the 'Banks'. It is an excellent run to make the 'Banks' in 18 days. Steerage passengers, at least some of their wives, had very strange ideas about the banks—supposed that they were dry land. One wife said to her husband in the morning when she heard where we were—'Jamie, Jamie rise man an' gang for a pailfu' o' fresh water, that we may get some things washin' wi't'. This was told very graphically by our old friend 'Johnthan'. Have run about 200 miles over the banks.

Friday 22 August. Passed a good many fishing vessels. Some of them French. I believe none are allowed to fish on the Banks of Newfoundland but the British and French. At twelve noon sounded—40 fathoms. Wind six points out of our course. About 100 miles from Newfoundland.

Saturday 23 August. Rainy morning—passed a number of fishing vessels. About twelve noon a fine breeze sprang up. Running from 9 to 10 knots on the right course. Spoke the *Heroine*[22] of Aberdeen on her homeward bound passage, but as the wind was blowing fresh, got time only to say report us 'All well' and gave her three cheers. Several pedestrian matches[23] took place this evening.

Sunday 24 August. A heavy rain this morning, which continued till mid-day. In consequence of which and a fresh breeze springing up, no public service took place. I had my school in the evening. The scholars did well and were rewarded as usual. The passengers kept pretty much below today.

Monday 25 August. A headwind. Lost way. About 40 miles from St Peter's Newfoundland and 100 from St Paul's. The latter an island with two lights, which lies in the main entrance to the Gulf of St Lawrence, between Cape Ray at the south west extremity of Newfoundland and Cape North, near the northern extremity of Cape Breton Island. This island is nearly 2 miles long and 1 broad. The only inhabitants are two men in charge of a depot of provisions, for the relief of shipwrecked persons, supported by the government of New Brunswick. From the position of this island ships make for it upon entering the gulf.

Tuesday 26 August. A strong headwind from the west this morning, accompanied with rain. About 12 noon it increast to a perfect hurricane with torrents of rain. None of the passengers remained on deck but myself. But it was so terrifically grand that I could not refrain look[ing] at the mighty waves, which you would have thought, as they rolled towards the ship and dashed against her in heavenly majesty, were ready to swallow us up alive. We were fully trimmed under storm sails, and having plenty of sea room I did not feel the least uneasy. The hurricane did not last above two hours. Some amusing scenes I am told took place in the steerage during the gale; the passengers were all closed up—pots, pans, trunks, tables, chairs etc. were breaking adrift, and tumbling from side to side in the ship. The pasengers obliged to sit down on the floor, and *hold on*—the one by the other, and allow these various articles to tumble over and over them. A large barque in view after the gale with foretop mast carried away.

Wednesday 27 August. Light breeze right ahead. A number of fishing vessels around us riding at anchor. Expecting to see land soon. The 20th day since we lost sight of the Flannel Islands—have made no way today—very cold night.

Thursday 28 August. Land ho! Land ho! was the cry this morning. The Island of Cape Breton was full in view when I got up. We came pretty near to it. Presents a high rocky shore. In the afternoon saw the Scalting Islands, a cluster running out from Cape Breton. Take your map and find me out—have made only 21 miles the last 24 hours.

Friday 29 August. Wind still right ahead. We have put about ship almost every watch, that is, every 4 hours. This piece of nauticalship was a novelty to me and at night makes a landsman start. Here it is—

Captain—Put the helm down.

Man at helm—Helm down.

Captain—Ease off jib sheets and fore sheets. Hard a lee.

The whole sailors pass the word.

Captain—Tacks and sheets.

Captain—Mainsail haul.

Captain—Forebow line let go and haul.

These operations bring the vessel upon the opposite tack. The coast of Newfoundland is now in view, it looks high and rocky like Cape Breton.

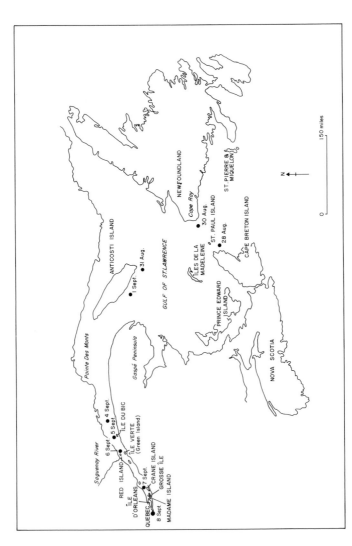

Map 3   The voyage of the *Lord Seaton* through the Gulf of St Lawrence to Quebec, 28 August — 8 September 1845, according to approximate positions given in Muir's Diary.

2 THE ST LAWRENCE

Saturday 30 August. The wind shifted about one this morning and have made a good run, entered the Gulf of St Lawrence about 9 am within 10 miles of Cape Ray. I may here mention that the mouth of the Gulf is about 55 miles 'twixt the Capes Breton and North. The Island of St Paul lies 'twixt the two capes in the main entrance of the Gulf and is the point which ships steer for. It is about 3 miles long by 1 mile broad. It is partially wooded with dwarf trees. The only inhabitants are the keepers of two lighthouses.

Sunday 31 August. In view of the Island of Anticosti. As it was blowing hard today [we] had sermon below in the steerage. I held my school in the cabin— saw a large ship on shore upon the Island of Anticosti, but as it was blowing hard could render her no assistance. This is an uninhabited island. And I shall here give an outline of Captain Bayfield R.N.'s description of it.[24] Anticosti—situated in the entrance of the N W arm of the Gulf—is 122 long 30 in extreme breadth and about 270 in circumference—shores of secondary limestone—near the coast is covered with thick, and often impenetrable forest of dwarf spruce, with gnarled branches so twisted and matted together that a man may walk for a considerable distance on their summits. The interior of the island is less sterile but trees do not grow to any size. Birds very scarce, probably because there are but few wild fruits for their support. Even the common Canadian Partridge or wood grouse to be found almost anywhere else is said not to exist upon this island. It is said there are only four or five species of quadrupeds, namely the black bear, fox, otter, marten and a few mice. The summers are cold, wet and foggy. Frosts commence in August, and in some severe seasons occur in every month of the year. Scarce any kind of grains would ripen here, except oats and barley in the more sheltered situations. Potatoes are destroyed by the early frosts. Abundance of small streams of excellent water—and many of these streams abound with salmon and trout. There is no good harbour around the whole island. The people in charge of the lighthouses, and provision posts and one man at Fox Bay are the only resident inhabitants. The provision posts have been established by the government and legislature of Lower Canada for relief of the crews of vessels shipwrecked upon the island. The ship *Granicus* was wrecked on this coast in November 1828 and the whole crew and passengers perished for want of food after enduring the most horrible misery. This caused the erection of the provision posts.[25]

Monday 1 September. A strong wind right ahead beating off Anticosti. Rather disagreeable from the rolling of the vessel— have been reading Bayfield's sailing directions for the river and Gulf of St Lawrence, very interesting at the present moment as I feel myself within its raging. It appears to be a more dangerous navigation than I was aware of. The greatest attention and watchfulness are necessary on the part of the Captain. And we have one of that description which keeps us all comfortable in our minds.

Tuesday 2 September. The wind now right astern. This has been one of the finest days we have had. The sea is as smooth as oil, and running along the Canadian Coast, at the rate of 5 knots, not the least perception of motion in the cabin. Every one in such good spirits, that a concert and ball were the evening's amusements. The *natural* flow of spirits sufficient to animate us without any *artificial* stimulant; which is prohibited by our worthy captain, at least disencouraged by him.

Wednesday 3 September. The wind has been fair all night. Running at 8 knots, but the weather is thick and foggy, and we must amuse ourselves the best way we can *within doors*.

Thursday 4 September. Fine morning, but wind right ahead. Pilot came on board 150 miles from Quebec. He is a very intelligent kind of man. He is a French Canadian. Can't read

English. Says he has three farms on the River de Loup. I shall here give you a short account of the St Lawrence Pilots. There are about 300 of them. They are strictly looked after. They are paid 18/- or 20/- for every foot of water the vessel draws for pilotage. They meet vessels as far down the river as Point des Monts, 300 miles below Quebec. They are suspended for three years if they go below that point. They pay 5 per cent of their earnings into a fund for behoof their widows and aged men, who receive about £25 year. They must be 7 years an apprentice and go 3 voyages to England and undergo an examination before being admitted. The captain has no more charge of the vessel after the pilot comes on board till she is moored at Quebec.

Friday 5 September. Beautiful morning with light breezes— opposite 'Bich Island'—about three miles long and one broad. There is a lighthouse upon it. The ship *Wm Dawson*[26] of Alloa is alongside of us. Has some passengers. She came through the Pentland Firth with us. Both sides of the river now fully in view. The land is what is called 'high rolling land', that is hills and valleys alternately like the waves in the midst of the 'Western Ocean'. Little cleared on the north side. On the south a number of French Canadian settlements are seen. Passed 'Point Mille Vaushe':[27] two ships were lost upon it last season, the whole crew of the one and the captain (Rae of Aberdeen)[28] of the other perished. A strong current runs here at the rate of 2 1/2 miles per hour. Have seen a number of seals today and white 'Puff Dunters'. In sight of 'Green Isle'—about 10 miles ahead— a long narrow island lying near the south side of the river—a light house on the north end of it.[29] Have got into the tide way and are drifting backwards.

Saturday 6 September. Have made little progress during the night—nearly opposite 'Saguenay River' at 12 noon. This river resembles a long and narrow mountain loch for about 50 miles up. It is nearly 2 miles broad filling up a deep transverse valley through mountains of *granite*. These mountains rise more or less abruptly from the water forming in some parts precipitous headlands, more than 1000 feet in height, which altho' wild barren is yet full of grandeur and beauty. Saguenay really is a

3 QUEBEC, seen from across the St Lawrence. Muir's ship anchored in the river on the evening of 8 September

remarkable and extraordinary river. At the entrance there is a bar across, on which there is from 18 to 20 fathoms of water, but immediately within, that depth increases to upwards of *100* fathoms! and further up for a distance of many miles it is fully 145 fathoms. It is this enormous depth, its mountainous shores, and its impetuous stream, that have rendered the Saguenay so celebrated and that entitle it to be classed among the most remarkable features in the geography of the Canadas. The bed of this river for many miles is sunk more than 100 fathoms below that of the Saint Lawrence at their point of junction—so that if the waters of the St Lawrence were to fall sufficiently to lay its bed dry, there would still remain a depth of more than 100 fathoms in the Saguenay. There is a small island near to it called 'Red Isle';[30] number of seals lying upon it. There is a very dangerous ridge of rocks extending from it for about 2 miles, all covered at flood tide. Here many vessels run in thick weather. One from Lerwick[31] was lost upon it in 1841. All on board perished. The *Brilliant*[32] of Aberdeen stuck upon them, but got clear off. 12 noon, have been lying at anchor with other 2 vessels since 8.06. Have seen a few white porpoises today. It is said white ones are not to be seen in any other part, except in the river and gulf. Had some dealings this forenoon with a French Canadian. He came alongside of us in his boat—he had fresh herrings and mutton. We purchased the leg of mutton for 2/4d and got 15 herrings for the shilling sterling. The herrings had not the taste of ours—something resembling a fresh water trout. Weighed anchor at 10 pm and got as far as 'Brandy Pots'—so called from the appearance of the water.

Sunday 7 September. Weighed anchor this morning about 8 am—had a fair wind up the river until 2 pm when it commenced to blow hard with heavy rain, and very thick, hardly seeing land. The wind soon commenced to blow a perfect hurricane with torrents of rain and continued the whole night— we brought up about 8 pm under 'Crane Isle' a little below the Quarantine Station where we anchored. The wind, which fortunately for us was right aft, and the tide which was running at 5 knots, were carrying us at a most prodigious rate, fully faster than a steamer. From the violence of the wind and the density of the rain the pilot had much difficulty in keeping the

4   PRESCOTT GATE, QUEBEC. Muir, landing on 10 September, described the steep and narrow streets rising from the harbour before he entered the fortified part of the city through this gate

narrow channel, which is only about a mile broad in some parts—each side of the channel being full of sunk rock. We passed within a few yards of a sunk rock which at times pops its head above water, where the *Rob Roy*[33] of Aberdeen went down with 300 passengers, when all perished. When the storm was at its fiercest we passed two poor fellows in a boat that had somehow or other been drifted from a vessel we passed riding at anchor. They cried to us to save them. We prepared a rope, but they were too far off, and we could turn our vessel neither to the right hand nor to the left at the time. They must very soon have perished—despair was in their countenances. The pilot says this was the severest gale he had experienced for the last 22 years. We were storm rigged, and required two men at the helm—but we had a steady captain, and crew, and an experienced pilot which made me the more easy, altho' I was not insensible to the great danger we were running. With feelings of the greatest gratitude and thankfulness I went to bed about 11 o'clock, our vessel riding with both anchors down, the gale still blowing hard. One vessel drifted ashore during the night. I should like to know if the storm was felt at Loirston.

Monday 8 September. Weighed anchor about 6 am. Rose early—beautiful morning—entered the Quarantine Station[34] about 22 miles below Quebec. You will understand every ship with passengers must anchor here until a Dr comes on board and inspects the ship and passengers, and then he gives the captain a bill of health or otherwise as the case may be. We were a '*clean* ship' and soon got under way. An Irishman[35] alongside of us was ordered into 'quarantine'. We're now slowly sailing up river. Have a fine view of each side of it. Thickly dotted with houses all painted or whitewashed, having well cultivated fields behind the same. Since leaving the Quarantine Station we have passed Grosse Island 1 1/4 miles long—Madame Island 2 miles long—and we are now opposite the Isle of Orleans. It is 18 miles long, with an extreme breadth of 5 miles. This appears a beautiful fertile island. It rises gradually from generally steep banks to the central elevation of about 500 feet above the water. It seems within a few miles of Quebec.

5   THE CITADEL OF QUEBEC, visited by Muir on 10 September—in pouring rain!

3 QUEBEC

9 o'clock at night. We are now moored within the harbour of Quebec, having made our run in 35 days[36]—and as I have kept my promise to you by writing something for you every day I shall say little more in this letter—and commence my next from this date giving you some account of my wanderings through America. I have not yet been ashore. I intend to remain in Quebec until Saturday the 13th and then to proceed to Montreal where I will remain for a few days. I will then proceed to Mr Findlay at Cumberland by Bytown,[37] and remain till the 10th of October—and then proceed to my brother at Nichol District by Elora.[38]

Harbour of Quebec

Tuesday 9 September. Our vessel being in the middle of the river did not get landed 'till afternoon—a considerable bustle on board, in consequence of the passengers preparing for landing, or rather for having their 'household' transferred on board a steamer for Montreal, which sailed the same evening with them. Before leaving the *Lord Seaton*, the passengers convened and publicly thanked Captain Talbot for his kindness. The old man Sanders Mitchell[39] mentioned in my last was their mouth piece. An acknowledgement to the same effect signed by all the adult passengers was presented to the Captain and inserted in the *Quebec Gazette*.[40] Each passenger took a copy to send home to their friends to let them know of their safe arrival. When the valedictory cheer was given some even shed tears. In the afternoon I went on shore with the Captain, and visited part of the town. As I was to remain but two days in Quebec the Captain kindly requested that I would return on board at night, and not remove my luggage until I started for Montreal. I did so.

6   VIEW FROM THE CITADEL OF QUEBEC. Muir judged this view of the harbour and river 'splendid'

Quebec

Wednesday 10 September. Heavy rains—went up to the castle or citadel in the morning with Captain Talbot. This fortress is held to be impregnable—had 'Montcalm' remained within its ramparts instead of coming forth to fight the British on the Plains of Abraham,[41] where he and the brave Wolfe fell together, no intrepidity or bravery on the part of the British could have dislodged him from his stronghold, but he accepted a challenge from General Wolfe to come forth and fight the British upon the plains and was conquered. The last and only other attempt upon this fortress was at the period of the American revolution in 1776, by Generals Montgomery and Arnold, two American Generals. It is said the attack was made with great courage and impetuosity. General Montgomery and nearly all his personal staff were killed. Arnold was wounded, and with most of his followers taken prisoner.[42] About half way up the almost perpendicular rock, and immediately beneath the citadel, is placed a board, with the following writing in large characters upon it. 'Here fell General Montgomery [   ] 1776'. I presume the British government has allowed this board to be placed and kept where it is to shew a bold attempt of a brave enemy. The citadel occupies the highest point of what is called Cape Diamond, it is elevated 350 feet above the river St Lawrence, and presents almost perpendicular cliffs towards the water. The view of the river and harbour from the citadel is splendid. Descending from the citadel, the streets and roads being bad, we hired a caleshe,[43] went to the battle ground upon the Plains of Abraham. A column or stone pillar is erected on the spot where the general is said to have been killed, but it is much defaced by idle people throwing stones at it. I believe, chiefly, by our own sailors on Sunday. This pillar is the only distinctive mark of the battle now remaining—strangers are shewn the place where Wolfe landed and drew up his guns, which was thought an extraordinary feat from the height and steepness of the cliffs. The place is now called Wolfe's Cove. We next visited that portion of the town called the suburbs of St Roch, which had been, a few weeks before, completely burned down by two separate fires;[44] and a more complete sweep of that destructive element could not be conceived, for nearly a mile in one direct course you saw nothing but stalks of chimneys

7 WOLFE'S COVE, QUEBEC, showing the cliffs up which Wolfe drew up his guns before the battle on the Plains of Abraham. Seen by Muir from the river on 11 September

standing like a forest of 'stumps'. The houses being all of wood save the chimneys were consumed to ashes, and so rapid was the burning that little or no property was saved. Many invalids actually perished, before they could be removed. Temporary booths are erecting for the more destitute, those who may be able to rebuild their houses are living and messing with friends. The benevolent public I have no doubt will come down liberally—and ultimately, this calamity will prove a benefit to the town, in many respects, as most great fires in towns do prove. It is singular how one house was preserved, whilst every other on both sides of it was consumed, but it was accounted for by a sudden shift of the wind which took place, and although it saved this house was the cause of many others being destroyed. A nunnery was likewise preserved, after it was on fire; or rather the fire ceased to burn, probably from the same cause the house above mentioned was saved, but full credence to its preservation was attributed to the prayers of the nuns. My fellow passenger Mr Gordon's brother's[45] house was burned to the ground and the last house that was burned. But how little did he expect, in the course of a forenoon, to be visited with such a calamity,— he went to his counting house as usual after breakfast—and his wife went to the other quarter of the town on a visit to a friend, whilst there someone reported that there was another great fire in the west suburbs just broken out—she remarked that she was thankful it was so far from her house, nearly a mile though in the same suburbs—but mark her surprise on her way home she learned her house was on fire. And before she reached it nothing could be saved. She had only been a few weeks married, and all, all was gone! save her husband—who had just been there in time to save a horse. He scarce knew whether his wife was safe or not till she made her appearance. After spending the evening with Mr Talbot I returned with him on board the *Lord Seaton*— on nearing the vessel the captain discovered that his men or most of them were in drink—and was about to hold an enquiry as to the cause, as he never allowed his men to get drunk, when I was obliged to plead for them and to inform him that I had given them a gallon of brandy in the morning to drink success to the *Lord Seaton*—which was the fact. Tomorrow I shall give you an account of Quebec and the vicinity as far as comes under my observation.

Thursday 11 September. This morning despatched letters and papers for Scotland—in the forenoon went out with Captain Talbot, Mr and Mrs Gordon and others to Charlesburgh, a place belonging to Mr Clerihue[46] formerly of Aberdeen, Mr Gordon's father-in-law, where we dined. This was the first *land* view I had of Canada and I was well pleased with it. Mr Clerihue's farm was well cultivated and had all the appearance of comfort to be expected, even at an Englishman's fireside. But Mr Clerihue is understood to be a man of property, and I therefore do not expect similarity. Besides Quebec is an ancient city and its suburbs ought to be much better cultivated than any other part of the province. Several pretty and neat country residences are in the vicinity of town, most of them are of wood and painted white, which gives them a cleanly appearance, and from the situation of Quebec are seen at a considerable distance. On landing at Quebec you have to wind your way up through steep, narrow and tortuous streets with still narrower alleys on both sides till you reach the fortified line or barrier. When you enter what is called Prescott Gate you see the New Parliament House, a very fine building with a lofty cupola. A little farther on you come to the English and French cathedrals, the Government Offices and Palace of Justice. Passing by these and *continually* ascending for about half a mile beyond, you reach the ramparts and gates on the upper side of the city. The town is very irregular, arising in some measure from the steepness of the ascent from the river to the plain above. There are few good private dwellinghouses, that is to say possessing architectural beauty, most of them are of rough hewn stone. A good many in the suburbs (St Roch) are now being rebuilt after the burning, with brick.

Quebec is 350 miles up from the sea. The St Lawrence is 3 miles in breadth immediately, or rather a little below the town and narrows into about a mile in breadth abreast of the Citadel; having in both these parts sufficient depth of water for the largest ships in the world—a rise and fall of 20 feet in its tides—and space enough in its capacious basin between Cape Diamond on the one hand and the Isle of Orleans on the other to afford room and anchorage for a thousand sail of vessels at a time, sheltered from all winds and perfectly secure. The chief trade is the lumber trade to the British market, and flour. The population according to the census published in May 1844 of the City and County of Quebec was

City	—32,876
County	—12,800
	45,676

of this number 36,371 are Roman Catholics
              5,494 are Church of England
              2,569 are Church of Scotland

and the remainder are in connection with various other denominations. Much more would require to be said of this ancient city but history will give you every information regarding it and little or no incident has occurred to myself worthy of being recorded. After dining with Captain Talbot I took my passage for Montreal, a distance of 180 miles, which cost me 6/- including a comfortable bed and provisions—deck passengers are charged only sixpence!—so much for opposition [sic]. Mr Gordon (my fellow passenger) having got a situation in Montreal, he and his brother went as passengers. The company was agreeable and many of them invited me to spend a day with them as I passed up the country. I left Quebec about 5 o'clock in the afternoon. The evening was beautiful and as I passed my little barque which wafted me across the Atlantic, the sailors gave me three cheers which caused a little curiosity, as I afterwards learned, who I might be, and this was heightened by my dress, having on a large plaid, which drew much attention and no small admiration.

Voyage from Quebec to Montreal

After we left Quebec, Wolfe's Cove 2 miles above the city was the first interesting spot to strangers. Here the lamented Wolfe landed with his gallant army in 1759, and ascended to the Plains of Abraham, where he fell a victim to his heroic enterprise. Many other places were pointed out as we passed up the river but the night, although full moon, drew the curtains so close that little could be seen from the centre of the river, and about 12 o'clock I rested a few hours upon my bed and was again upon deck by 4 o'clock on.

Friday 12 September—when I found myself upon Lake St Peter 50 miles below Montreal. This Lake is but an expansion of the river, about 25 miles long and 12 to 15 miles wide, while the average breadth of the river proper from Quebec to Montreal is about 2 miles. In addition to the more customary forms of craft usually employed in the navigation of large rivers, I was much struck with the enormous timber rafts, which I saw upon the St Lawrence, borne along on their way to market either by the force of the current, or huge oars called sweeps aided by a number of small sails. These floating islands of timber with huts here and there rising from their low surface, for the accommodation of the raft men, have a very grotesque appearance.[47]

8 MONTREAL, reached by Muir on the morning of 13 September. He was 'very much pleased' with its 'clean appearance'

4 MONTREAL

Nothing particular occurred on the passage and after a pleasant trip and comfortable breakfast I arrived safe at Montreal at about 8 o'clock and put up at Orrs Hotel, Notre Dame Street.[48] Spent this day in visiting the Town, met with Mr Peter Nichol from Aberdeen,[49] with whom I spent the evening.

Saturday 13 September. After breakfast called upon Mr Auljo[50] formerly of Aberdeen to whom I have a letter of introduction from his brother-in-law, Dr Jamieson.[51] Dined with Mr A at Rasco's Hotel[52]—one of the largest establishments in Montreal—nearly a hundred ladies and gentlemen dined at the Table all in the French style. A Bill of Fare is issued every day. The following is the bill for the day on which I dined, Saturday September 13, 1845:

1. Soups
   Oxtail
   Macaroni
2. Fish Bass au Gratin
3. Entrees
   Cotellettes d'Agneau aux Concombres
   Ris de Veau Piques, Sauce Tomate
   Croquettes de Volaille
   Queues de Boeuf
   Fricasée de Poulet, à la Chevalière
   Chartreuses de Gibier
   Risolles de Poulet
   Poitrines de Mouton Grillées, Sauce Piquante
   Boeuf Braisé aux Légumes
4. Roast
   Beef
   Turkey
   Ducks
   Mutton

5   Dessert Italian Cream
    Rice Pudding
    Puffed Fritters
    Custard Pudding
    Prune Tarts
    Wine Jelly
    Génoises au Gros Sucre
    etc. etc. etc.
Wines

		$	c
Madeira—	Blackburn/very old	$	c
	No 1	2	—
	No 2	1	50
Do	Howard March & Co	1	75
Do	Lamby (very old)	2	—
Do	Smith, Bailey & Co	1	50
Port—	Table in draft	1	—
	Austect, Bottled in 1834	1	50
	Superior DO	2	—
Claret—	Chateau Lafitte	2	50
	Do No 2	2	—
	Latour	2	—
	Larose	2	—
	St Julien	1	—
	Vin de Bordeaux		60
Champagne—	Nuinvart Père et Fils	2	—
	Perrier Jouet et Cie	2	—
	Cordon Bleu	2	—
Sherry—	Table in Draft	1	—
	Duff Gordon & Co	1	50
	Triate Gold	2	—
	Lobo Pale	2	50
	Smith Bailey & Co	2	—
Rhine Wine—	Sparkling Hock	2	—
	Rudesheimer	2	—
	Niersteimer	2	—
	Johannisberg	2	50
Burgundy—	Chambertin	2	—
	Barsac	1	—
	Sauterne Emericon	1	50
Liqueurs—	Maraschino		
	Curacao	10 cents	
	Absinth	per glass	
	Kirchenwasser		

Immediately after dinner the whole party rose from table excepting a few gentlemen who had friends dining with them, who remained at their wine till the ladies returned to the same room to tea. The rate of living at this hotel is seven dollars per week or £1.8.-d sterling, and this includes bed and board. Visited both Houses of Parliament this morning, but as the session was not sitting had not the pleasure of seeing or hearing any of the members.

Sunday 14 September. The rain particularly heavy this morning, such as seldom to be seen in Scotland, but I was told common here at certain seasons. Forenoon went to the Roman Catholic Cathedral.[53] Heard high mass. This is the first time I ever witnessed this Romish rite and to my mind the whole ceremony was, to say the least of it, a most unmeaning thing. The altar is very large, I numbered upwards of *100*! within the railing or stage, in front of the altar piece. The ornaments upon and about the altar were many—rich and massive—the High Priest and the whole persons dramatic were dressed each according to their office. It reminded me very much upon a pantomime performance. After the morning service (which was gone through in French) I went down near to the altar. Immediately upon my right hand was the Black Nuns, about seventy in number. They are so called from their dress. Their upper garment being a loose black frock or gown, something like our ministers' pulpit gown—a black hood over a white muslin cap or mutch, resembling our fish wives' *gipsies*, and a small white handkerchief round the shoulders. Some of the young ones were good looking, particularly about a dozen of them who were only under probation or upon trial, and were differently and neatly dressed. The Grey Nuns, so called from their dress, sat upon the opposite side of the church, but at too great a distance to discover how they looked in comparison with their *black* sisters. After leaving the cathedral I went and heard a Mr Arnott[54] from Glasgow—he was preaching in a wooden church in connection with the sympathizers (Frees). I thought nothing of him, altho' much spoken of *here*. In the afternoon I went to the English Cathedral.[55] The congregation was thin. Heard a most excellent discourse. The music was most delightful. I think the organist was an Aberdeen lady, a Jane Wetherburn. Dined

9   THE ST LAWRENCE AT MONTREAL. 'Montreal has no feature which charms the visitor as much as the promenade along its edge of the quays'

at 6 o'clock with Mr Peter Nicol—Mr James Nicol,[56] [the] advocate's brother.

Monday 15 September. Not having got a proper view of my friends the Grey Nuns yesterday, I paid a visit to their establishment this morning, to which the public are freely admitted, as well as to the others in this City, excepting what is now called 'Maria Monks Nunnery', from the very extra-ordinary excitement caused by a publication[57] made in that Lady's name, of the doings *within*. When I knocked at the door an elderly female presented herself, and having expressed a wish to visit the establishment she kindly invited me in and shewed me over the whole house. Here are kept, an hospital for old men. One for a similar class of females, also two schools, one for boys and another for girls. These children are what the nun called *foundlings*, being either orphans, or left destitute and deserted by their parents. They were all taught in the French language—some of the girls were very neat handed and were (many of them) employed at fancy work. After receiving their education the boys and girls are placed out as servants, and the like. It was the dinner hour when I visited—the dinner con-sisted of soup, bread and beef. Three nuns waited upon each hospital or class of inmates, and distributed the meat. The nuns very freely and readily entered into conversation about their establishment. Few could speak English—the French only being spoken. There is a very neat chapel attached to the nunnery, all hung round with pictures—no sooner did I enter than my guide prostrated herself before one of the pictures, and in that position continued with her hands clasped, during the time I was viewing the chapel and the pictures. She was no doubt invoking the Virgin on behalf of the heretic who was sacrilegiously treading the sanctified ground of pure and virgin nuns and holy priests. Upon my returning to the door of the chapel she rose and crossed herself and said there was nothing more to be seen. I then put a piece of money into her hand, for which she politely thanked me, and having conducted me to the same door which I entered, bade me good morning—spent the remainder of the day visiting different parts of the town. Drank tea in the evening with Mr Allan, [the] advocate's uncle.[58]

10 THE CATHEDRAL, MONTREAL. Muir remarks on the 'towering grandeur' of the 'French' or Roman Catholic cathedral, and on how it dominated views of the city from the surrounding country—see illustration 8 above

Tuesday 16 September. Mr Peter Nicol having set out this morning on a tour to the Falls of Niagara I accompanied him by stage as far as the village of Lachine about 9 miles up the St Lawrence and where the River Ottawa joins it. I returned to Montreal in the afternoon by the banks of the St Lawrence. There is no water conveyance on the St Lawrence twixt Montreal and Lachine in consequence of dangerous rapids called the Lachine Rapids, so it may be said that Montreal is at the head of the free navigation *by steam* upon the St Lawrence, but a canal is presently forming which will overcome this obstacle and will thus extend the navigation by steam, both by the Ottawa and St Lawrence, for many hundred miles westward.[59] Spent the evening with some gentlemen at my lodgings [in] Oshacknacy St.[60]

Wednesday 17 September. Took a drive round the 'mountain' with Mr Auldjo this forenoon, dined with Mr Andrew his son-in-law and the other branches of Mr Auldjo's family, being a meeting of friends upon the occasion of Miss Richardson's marriage, a near relative.[61] The Misses Auldjo[62] are very accomplished young ladies beautiful players upon the piano. Mr Auldjo accompanied me to my lodgings, had a glass together—it being my intention to leave tomorrow morning. I shall now give you a description of Montreal as far as came under my own observation, and such statistics as I have been able to pick up during my short stay in this very pleasant and delightful capital of the United Provinces of Lower and Upper Canada. But as this will occupy two or three pages of 'my log' I shall close for the night and resume tomorrow when I get my foot on board the Ottawa steamer.

Thursday 18 September. Having taken my passage yesterday from Montreal to 'Bytown' a distance of 120 miles, and for which I paid a sovereign, I started this morning at 7 o'clock by stage as far as the village of Lachine, which as I mentioned before lies at the mouth of the Ottawa or Grand River. And being now embarked on board one of the River Steamers[63] which plys twixt the St Lawrence and Bytown, where I find I shall have to remain for the next twenty-four hours, I shall now, according to promise last night, give you a brief history of

11   THE INTERIOR OF THE CATHEDRAL, MONTREAL. Here on 14 September heard High Mass 'a most unmeaning thing', 'a pantomime performance'!

Montreal and then proceed with my journey from the point where I now am—near to St Annes, rendered famous by Moore's celebrated Canadian Boat Song.[64] The distance of Montreal from Quebec is 180 miles, but although that distance would be considered great in Scotland it is thought nothing of here. The many splendid steamers which daily navigate the noble river St Lawrence, the cheapness of the fares—and the magnificence of the scenery induce many a one to take a trip between these two cities, which is accomplished in about thirty hours, giving some time to visit the places on shore.

The City of Montreal is at present the first in population and commercial importance in our American possessions. It is the capital of the United Provinces of Lower and Upper Canada. It extends along the River St Lawrence for about two miles, the wharfs extending nearly the whole distance. On approaching almost from any quarter this place appears to great advantage. The towering grandeur of the French Cathedral, the spires of other churches and the numerous well built houses, all with their bright and shining tiled roofs, give the traveller a very favourable impression of the city. The finest view which I had of the city was from Mount Royal,[65] a hill which rises about one mile from the town to a height of 550 feet, forming a prominent object in the picture from every point of view, and, being dotted with country seats and ornamentally wooded, adds much to the picturesque beauty of the scene.

The public buildings are rather numerous and imposing for a place of its size, now numbering about 45,000 inhabitants. The Roman Catholic Cathedral is said to be the most magnificent structure of its kind in America. It can be seen for many miles rising in majestic grandeur above all other buildings by which it is surrounded. I ascended the tower to the top, a height of 250 feet, by a flight of steps. The view is grand, the city appears as it were a considerable way beneath you, the whole suburbs are in view and the River St Lawrence for a considerable distance both above and below the town. The surrounding country is also seen to a great distance, the high mountains in the state of Maine U.S. closing in the back ground. This edifice was commenced in 1824, and according to a description of it put into your hands as you ascend the tower, opened for public worship on the 15th of July 1829. It is designed in the pointed

Gothic style of the Middle Ages. Its length is 255 feet and its breadth 134 feet: the two front towers being 220 feet in height. It can seat 10,000 persons with comfort there being 1244 pews— there [are] as yet few ornaments or pictures inside, and the inside of the towers has to be finished, but every person is charged 1/6d who ascends and a great deal of money will soon be collected for completing this part of the building.

I was very much pleased with the clean appearance of Montreal, the whole of the town appeared to be new; and on making the remark I was informed that it had been wholly rebuilt within the last twelve or fifteen years, but the streets are rather narrow, the houses in general having been built upon the former site, which is to be regretted as foot passengers in wet weather are much annoyed with the mud flung from the vehicles which are generally driven very fast along the street. The houses are all built of limestone, pick dressed, which I liked as well as our granite. There is at present erecting a public market, the dimensions of which I was not able to procure, but it is much larger and handsomer than our Aberdeen Market.[66]

The quay for the shipping at Montreal is much admired. A writer says 'The beauty and strength of its masonry far exceeds anything of the kind I have ever seen at home. It has no fellow in London, and the celebrated quay at Great Yarmouth is far its inferior. Dublin and Liverpool, both noted for fine quays, may have greater pretensions, but in one respect, that in Montreal has no equal. Below the level of the quay, probably 12 feet, there are most capacious wharfs, at whose sides vessels of the largest class can unload with ease and safety, which cannot be said either of Dublin or Liverpool. In fact Montreal has no feature which charms the visitor as much as the promenade along its edge of the quay'. These quays are just now extending still farther up the river joining with the Lachine Canal which is to be opened in a few days and thus completing the water communication both by the Ottawa and the St Lawrence to and from Montreal.

Island of Montreal

The City of Montreal is situated upon the north banks of the St Lawrence, and the island on which it stands is formed by the junction of the mouths of the Ottawa with the St Lawrence. This island, which is called Montreal, is said to be 28 miles in length, 10 miles in its greatest breadth, and about 70 miles in circumference. It chiefly belongs to a religious order of Catholics called the St Sulpicians. The fertility of this island is such as to give it the name of the 'Garden of Canada'—to which as far as I have yet seen it is justly entitled to. I shall now close this meagre account of Montreal and return to St Annes which I passed this morning, but from which I am now 100 miles distant up the River Ottawa—and I shall title this part of my log 'Rambles upon the Ottawa'.

12 JUNCTION OF THE OTTAWA AND ST LAWRENCE, where Muir embarked on a river steamer for Bytown on 18 September

5 THE OTTAWA RIVER

After embarking at Lachine this morning [18 September] nothing occurred to draw my attention till I came to St Annes 20 miles up the river. Here commences a succession of rapids and several small islands, which are somewhat difficult to navigate, and are only overcome by locks. The first lock we passed through, is said to be 45 feet wide and 180 feet long built of strong mason work. It was pointed out to me that these rapids, which are near to the village of St Annes, is the place where the poet Moore located the scenes of his Canadian Boat Song.

> Faintly as tolls the evening chime
> Our voices keep tune, and our oars keep time;
> Soon as the woods on the shore look dim,
> We'll sing at St Annes our parting hymn;
> Row Brothers Row, the stream runs fast
> The rapids are near and the day light's past.

After passing St Annes, which excited a considerable interest on board amongst the passengers, most of whom were lumber merchants originally from Ireland, we next came to the Lake of the Two Mountains, being an expansion of the Ottawa about 10 miles long and 8 miles wide. Two hills supposed to be elevated 400 or 500 feet above the river give the name to this lake. We passed close to the Two Mountains, where there is an Indian Village containing the remnant of two tribes called the Mohawk and Algonquins. I was very anxious to land here, which was a beautiful romantic spot, and the idea of the only inhabitants being the original tribes made me the more desirous, but I was advised by the captain not to do so. Here the river contracts in width to about half a mile giving you a distinct view of both sides but nothing is to be seen but wood. It soon again expands forming what is called the Upper Lake of the

Two Mountains—about 9 miles further west the river again contracts to about half a mile in width—here we passed a settlement called Rigaud—8 miles further on we landed at a small village called Carillon, where the steam navigation is interrupted by rapids, and took stage for 12 miles. The passengers required five coaches, which were in readiness at the landing place to convey them this distance. The drivers who were French Canadians, were the most fearless fellows I had ever met with in the way of driving. The road was excessively bad, in fact it could not be called a road—nothing but mud and mire. This, however, did not daunt the five postilions, each vying who should go ahead at the great risk of the passengers being tumbled into the mud. Having some ladies on the coach, and seeing our own peril, we put a stop to this furious driving by a little stratagem of getting ahead, and then causing our coach zig-zag the road as any of the others attempted to pass. We all arrived safe at a village called Grenville, where we again took steam.

The next stage we stopped at was a village called L'Original, about 18 miles farther up the river, but by this time it was becoming night and little more was to be seen, and finding the passengers pleasant and agreeable, I entered more freely into conversation with them, and was kindly invited by many of them to their houses. Amongst the passengers was a Mrs McNabb[67] a widow lady from whom I got a great deal of news—she had a daughter married to a grandson of the late Bailie Lyon of Inverurie[68]—that she had two brothers, students of medicine in Aberdeen[69] of the name of [   ] I remembered upon them. She also gave me an account of an old acquaintance Mrs Robertson[70] and her niece Jane Wedderburn, who married a Dr Gillie,[71] and afterwards a Mr McIntosh, a lawyer in Bytown,[72] and is again a widow and now plays the organ in an English church in Montreal. Many of the passengers did not seem inclined to 'turn in' at an early hour and we passed the time together till twelve o'clock when the captain came and told me that I could not be landed where I purposed, but they were come to a wharf[73] where they had to put out some goods and if I chose I might go ashore, as I could get a bed in a tavern not far off and could cross the river next morning by a canoe, when I should only have a few miles to travel to the place I

13　THE LAKE OF THE TWO MOUNTAINS on the Ottawa River, which Muir passed along in the river steamer on 18 September

purposed landing. Being told that we had sailed 100 miles up the river I landed and got my trunk on shore, but being very dark and no person having come to the steamer or to take any charge of the goods landed, I did not know very well where or which way to go, for I saw no light or house save a kind of building upon the end of the wharf which I soon discovered to be a store for depositing goods landed by the river craft. At last after having resolved to take up my quarters amongst the goods which had been landed, I observed at a little distance, down the river amongst some trees, something white, but not being as yet much accustomed with the appearance of Canadian taverns, was doubtful whether it was an inhabited house or not, but house of some kind I became certain it was—and having left my trunk at the landing place I went and reconnoitered, and going into what, (from a glimmering light from a few burned sticks) I thought was a bar room, tumbled over something, which from its growling and the shaggy feel I took for a bear, and expected to be instantly devoured alive. Feeling no immediate death like grasp from Old Bruin, I got up the best way I could, and getting some of the sticks kindled up I discovered four black ugly looking like devils lying upon the floor rolled up in buffalo skins. I called to them repeatedly but received no answer. I now found I was in a pretty large, solitary tavern upon the banks of the river. I next tried for the kitchen but could find no such place. I at last stumbled upon a room and saw from the window that there was an empty bed, and having marked my way downstairs, (for I was through the greater part of the house by this time) I returned to the wharf for my luggage, and having found the same room I barricaded the door with my trunk and the chairs, and having wrapped myself up in my large plaid, threw myself upon the bed where I slept soundly till 10 o'clock next morning. I should rather say this morning the 19th.

Friday 19 September. When I made my appearance this morning the landlady of the house was not a little surprised where I had come from, and how I had got into the house without any person hearing me. I soon explained matters— and having got a comfortable breakfast, I crossed to the south side of the river in a canoe, in search of my brother-in-law's

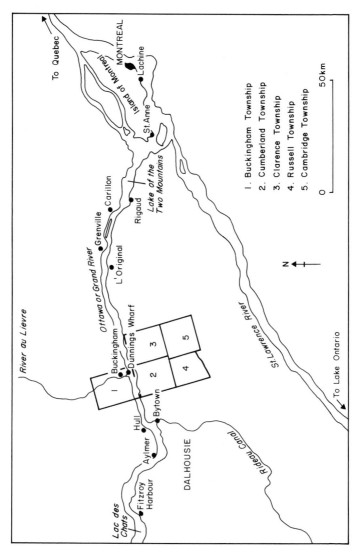

Map 4   Montreal and the Ottawa River, illustrating Muir's travels from 13 September to 8 October 1845.

place, which lay about 3 miles through the 'bush'. This was the first time I had been in the 'bush', and I must confess was a little uneasy, as I was made aware of the danger of taking the wrong course. However, I kept the 'blaze' and steered my course from one 'clearance' to another till, at last, I arrived at my friend's 'shanty'. I would not have known either my sister or her husband,[74] had I met them anywhere else, although they had been only 12 years 'out'. I found them pretty comfortable, but like most new settlers with a considerable deal to do, and little to do it with. Visited a few of the neighbouring settlers in the afternoon.

Note. 'Blaze' a mark upon the trees to point out the direct way to any particular clearance.

Saturday 20 September. Went over to a neighbour settler called Squire Cameron,[75] an old military officer, who had been in America since 1804, was in the war of 1812, and got a grant of land from the British Government, which he had disposed of and was now located in the bush upon the Ottawa. Apparently in reduced circumstances, but still retaining the Scotish spirit of independence— returned in the evening. Thunder and rain in the afternoon.

Sunday 21 September. A beautiful morning. Thermometer 68°. Went to church with my brother-in-law and his family, or rather to hear divine worship, the church having been destroyed by fire last year, and the new one was not finished.[76] The service was performed in a settler's house by a Mr Bell,[77] a very excellent preacher. The new church is built of stone upon a very romantic spot near to the Ottawa, but there are few settlers in this part of the country, and consequently the congregation is few, most of them came up to me and very kindly shook hands and asked me to their houses. Mr Pettree[78] the M.P. of the district, who lives in the neighbourhood, invited me to dine with him. Found him a very pleasant, and intelligent gentleman, his wife a very lady kind of woman with a beautiful young family, He lives upon a very romantic rising ground where he has built a neat framewood cottage surrounded on all sides with a veranda and the grounds laid out with much taste, and a fine garden producing all kinds of fruit in the open air, which requires the

fostering hand of the hothouse in this country [Scotland]. He
has a splendid view of the river for many miles. Returned in
the evening to Mr Findlay's. My niece, who accompanied me
as my guide, lost her way in the wood, it being very dark, and
our light went out. After wading through several swamps she
gained a clearance, and knew where she was. We soon reached
home, but we both got a pretty good fright, indeed I was more
so than she was, as we heard the wolves at no great distance,
but she said they would not touch us and it was so dark the
bears would not see to attack us!

Monday 22 September. I this day went through the 'bush'.
I think I have not explained to you what the 'bush', a 'clearance', or a 'shanty' mean, which I shall now briefly do. When
you say you are going into the 'bush' it means into a large wood
or I may say an interminable forest of the loftiest trees you
could imagine, from 50 to 150 feet high, and sometimes so thick
upon each other that you cannot penetrate through them, and
in some places you may travel days nay weeks or months before
coming upon a clearance or human dwelling, hence the great
danger of going far into the bush without a guide and a compass.
The settler when he has no [word illegible] goes into the bush
and commences cutting down the trees. The opening which he
makes is called a 'clearance' on which he builds a small square
house with the logs just as they are cut 'dove tailing' them at
the four corners. The roof is sometimes formed by scooping out
cedar trees, making the wall a little higher upon one side than
the other and these scooped trees form a kind of inclined plane
when laid upon the top of the wall something like tiles, and
thus carry off the water. Sometimes couples or rafters are raised
covered with thin pieces of cedar resembling in size our slates,
and which are called 'shingles'. The house is generally about
20 feet square, in which the whole family live and sleep without
any division. This is called living in a 'shanty'—the word shanty
or 'chantie' is from the French, signifying a small house. In such
houses as thus described, do the bushmen live for years until
their 'clearances' produce sufficient means to enable them to
enlarge. The settlers are very hospitable, and if you call near
nightfall, you are compelled to remain overnight, and partake
of their hospitality, which is generally pork, potatoes, boiled

apples and other kinds of preserved fruit, and tea. Tea is a standing dish and is used at every meal, and most frequently without sugar. I this night slept at a Mr Golightly's[79] who had been in the township for twelve years. He had got ahead of his neighbours. He had nearly 80 acres cleared, all done by himself and his sons. He was quite happy and comfortable. He and his wife were farm servants in the south of Scotland and had only about £30 when they started. They have now a farm of 200 acres all paid and 80 acres in regular rotation. Their house was the most comfortable and cleanly looking in the district, but still in rather a primitive state, there being only one division across the centre of the house, and in one of these divisions were arranged round the walls, three beds or couches, without curtains, or separation, one of which was occupied by the guid-man and his wife, another by their daughter and the third by myself. I was first to bed and last up.

Tuesday 23 September. Left my hospitable friend this morning after breakfast, and went to Dunnings Wharf, the place where I first landed, to enquire after my luggage which I had left behind me. In consequence of a wet day remained there all night, and amused myself the best way I could. Several Indians were encamped on the river side making canoes. I went into their tents and gave their children some halfpence. None of them could speak English, but expressed, by their gestures, apparent satisfaction. Went early to bed.

Wednesday 24 September. After breakfast walked about 5 miles up the east bank of the romantic river 'Aux Lièvres' until I came to a village called Buckingham, the principal town or place of the district of the same name. This river is about the size of the Dee[80] where it runs into the Ottawa, and besides its natural beauties, and romantic scenery, with its numerous cascades, rapids, and falls, which delight the senses, it possesses some of the most powerful natural waterfalls for the working of machinery that could be imagined. I was advised to go and visit Mr Bigelow's[81] Sawmills at Buckingham as the wonder of the place. I waited upon that gentleman, and although I had no introduction to him, he kindly invited me to dine with him, and afterwards showed me over his extensive works. He said his father came from the United States about 22 years ago, when the place was without an inhabitant, and that in consequence of his mills and that of another gentleman's, Mr Bowman, of a similar description upon the opposite side of the river, it had increased to upwards of 2,000. Mr Bigelow employs upwards of 250 labourers. He has 30 saws, which cut about 200 trees a day—chiefly into 3 inch 'plank' for the home market. The rapidity with which the large trees were transformed into these thin boards, and all of equal length was truly astonishing, and required some enquiry and inspection before it could be discovered. Great mechanical skill and ingenuity were displayed by this gentleman in taking every advantage of the natural powers of the water. He had his mill house (all of wood) and machinery so placed, and constructed, that the trees, after being floated down the river, and passing into a slip or basin which joined the mill, were, with the aid of one man, directed through a sluice, which ran them beneath the cross cut saw, and after being cut, were forwarded upon rollers attached to the machinery, and 'slabbed', from thence to the saws to be cut according to the thickness required. The slabs being of no value were dropped from the saw into the water which moved the large wheel and were carried down into the river. And the planks or boards as they were cut dropped into a sluice, and floated down a lead for nearly a mile to a place upon the banks of the river, where they could be conveniently rafted for the ports of Montreal or Quebec. Mr Bigelow has four large farms or tracts of land upon the river. The first is 23 miles distant, the next 40, another 80 and the highest 150—but these he keeps more for the lumber or timber trade, than for agricultural purposes. He has likewise about 60 yoke of oxen for drawing his lumber from the woods to the river during winter. I saw about 40 of his oxen in one field. They very much resemble the work oxen in use in this country about 40 years ago. All have large spreading horns. Mr Bigelow is an American and his wife the same from the State of New England. They have 5 young children. I was struck on observing two graves neatly enclosed in the garden in front of the house. On enquiry I was informed that it was the grave of a brother and of a child of Mr B. As I understood the country was very thinly peopled nor'ward, being within 300 miles of the Highlands of Hudson's Bay, and having no person with me I thought it best to retrace my steps, and before the sun went down I again found myself upon the north bank of the Ottawa, which I crossed, and steered my course the best way I could to my friends, where I arrived before it was dark. They were becoming alarmed about me, having been absent two days. The soil of the district of Buckingham is rather of a light sandy nature, and not much done in the way of agriculture. Enough for one day.

Thursday 25 September. Went over to my friend's Squire Cameron's to a 'logging bee'—I guess you will calculate that I should explain what a 'logging bee' is—this is the first of the kind I have seen, and may be briefly explained as a gathering of one's neighbours, with their horses and work oxen for the purpose of drawing the trees cut down into large piles for being burned previously to cropping the land. The master, or 'bos' as he is termed, provides meat and drink for man and beast, but no wages or other remuneration is expected, excepting a similar return. The bee generally ends with a dance, something like our 'claiks' or 'harvest home'. Got tea and returned home with Mr Findlay.

Friday 26 September. Went down to Dunnings Wharf, returned by Captain Petrie's where I drank tea, he showed me over his farm which consists of about 300 acres but not much more than the half of it cleared.

Saturday 27 September. Dined and spent the day with Captain Petrie.

Sunday 28 September. Went to hear sermon at the Church of Cumberland, where I was last Sunday along with Mr Findlay and his family. Went home, by the river, with Captain Petrie where I dined.

Monday 29 September. Left Cumberland this afternoon in order to go by the steamer to Bytown[82] but she did not make her appearance. I had to sit up all night watching her arrival, and having nothing else to fill up the next page I shall just note down what occurs to me, and what I have learned in reference to this locality. Cumberland is a Township lying upon the south bank of the Ottawa, consisting of about 62,000 acres, of which about 10,000 are settled, but not above 2,000 are cultivated. Cumberland, Clarence, Cambridge, and Russel form a county, called Russel, and returns one M. of Parliament—Mr Petrie is the present member, and as he lives in the district does much to improve the country, both in its civil and religious institutions. He is very enterprising and spirited; as yet there is no village or post office in the locality, but these will not now be long wanting, as Mr Petrie has succeeded in procuring a government grant of £4,000 for the purpose of forming a road along the south bank of the river, from Lachine 9 miles above Montreal to Bytown a distance of more than 100 miles, which will open up the country, and enable it to 'go ahead'. But I find this is more a lumbering than an agricultural district owing to the very high wages offered by the lumber merchants to active young woodcutters who will earn 20 dollars per month besides being 'found'. The land upon the banks of the Ottawa is various, and cannot be put down as first quality. The high and hard woodlands are partly sandy, and partly of a gravelly loam with limestone subsoil, having a clay bottom where swampy. A considerable quantity of limestone is seen in the surface after the ground is cleared. The kinds of timber are various, but chiefly pine, which denotes the poorest kind of land, but it is a curious fact that it is hardwood that springs up where pine has been cut.

Tuesday 30 September. The Steam Boat *Porcupine* from Montreal made its appearance this morning at 6 o'clock and I embarked from the same wharf on which I landed upon the night of the 18th, but much better acquainted with the people and locality on my leaving than on my arrival there. Having paid my fare at Montreal to Bytown with leave to stop by the way, I expected to have nothing more to pay, but a big bluff fellow of a captain, insisted that I should cash up cabin fare again, but I resisted the imposition, and we came to very high words. At last to end the matter I said I would pay deck fare and expose the company to the public before the end of the voyage. When he knew I had come from Captain Petrie's, he became very civil and requested me to go to my breakfast in the cabin. I gave him such an answer as I thought he deserved. I found he was an impudent Yankee. I arrived within the first lock of the Rideau Canal which divides the Upper and Lower Town of Bytown about 11 o'clock. The morning was beautiful and I had an excellent view of the natural romantic scenery up the river. The scenery as you approach Bytown becomes beautifully grand. One thinks he is entering upon the Highland Glens and waterfalls of Old Scotland. I drove to the Dalhousie Hotel—a very excellent house kept by a McDonald. From the boarding system and all feeding at the same table and sitting in one public room you may soon pick up acquaintances. I met with a Mr Christie,[83] a nephew of an old acquaintance of my own Dr Christie of Old Deer,[84] who introduced me to his wife, who likewise turned out to be an acquaintance, she being a daughter of a Mr Strachan sometime a farmer at Anguston, Deeside.[85] I spent the evening in their house and gave them all the news of the old country, with which they were much amused.

14 LOCKS ON THE RIDEAU CANAL, BYTOWN [OTTAWA], reached by Muir on the steam boat *Porcupine* on 30 September

6 BYTOWN [OTTAWA]

Wednesday 1 October. Visited different parts of the town today but shall not enter upon any description of the place till I am more aquainted with it—my impression is very favourable.

Thursday 2 October. A beautiful day, took a walk a few miles down the river, visited the Rideau Rapids and locks upon the Rideau Canal, met my steam boat acquaintance Mrs McNab going to Bytown, consequently did not go to her cottage as I intended—returned to dinner much pleased with what I had seen of this locality. The particulars afterwards. Called at the Royal Exchange Hotel, which is kept by Robertson Lyon, a son of the late Baillie Lyon of Inverury.[86] Was introduced to a Mr Sherriff[87] editor of the Bytown Gazette: 'Jamie Johnston'[88] as he was generally termed—he is the Member of Parliament for the County of Clarendon.[89] He is a most eccentric character, has a great deal to say, and when speaking in the 'House' is generally '*coughed* down'. I also met with the sheriff,[90] and a Mr Spark,[91] the chief holder of land in and about Bytown, and several other choice characters. We all went to see a dwarf[92] man without arms perform some wonder feats with his toes, the same as with his fingers—such as loading and firing a pistol, playing the violin, shooting with a bow and arrow, cutting fancy papers with a pair of scissors. I asked if he was married. He said he was and had three children. This created a good deal of amusement. Everybody was much pleased with the many extraordinary feats he performed, all with his legs and toes without anyone to assist him. After this exhibition we adjourned to a drinking shop and had a great deal of fun. A Captain Hunter,[93] another singular character, amused us with

15 THE OTTAWA RIVER AT BYTOWN. 'The scenery as you approach Bytown becomes beautifully grand. One thinks he is entering upon the Highland Glens and waterfalls of Old Scotland', enthused Muir on 30 September. What higher compliment could there be?

a number of beautiful airs upon the Irish pipes and also gave us some curious songs; being about a mile from the inn Mr Lyon kindly sent a carriage for us and I got to my lodgings by one o'clock in the morning.

Friday 3 October. There was a meeting today of the 'Dalhousie District Agricultural Society'[94]—and having been introduced to the chairman, Mr William Thomson,[95] and Captain Baker,[96] the secretary, and several of the members, I was appointed one of the judges of the livestock,[97] along with my old acquaintance Mr Gilbert Heron of Birness,[98] who has a farm in the vicinity of Bytown, and a Mr Francis Smith,[99] a lumber merchant with whom I became acquainted in the steam boat from Montreal. The exhibition (taking to account the infancy of this district) was very excellent, especially the saddle horses, the sheep and pigs, the last were superior to almost any I had ever seen at home. They have not yet begun to feed cattle in this district. The only cattle killed are oxen and cows after being unfit for use: of course the beef is not to be compared to ours, but still I was surprised at its sweetness, which I can account only for, from the nature of the wild woodland pasture, being rich and nutritious. The farmers are doing much to improve the breed of the cattle, but the long winter is much against the procuring of a sufficient quantity of turnips for rearing stock. But so long as hay and oats continue cheap this will not be so much felt. I was very much pleased with the saddle horses. They are of small size, remarkably swift. The horse is always allowed to remain 'entire' and not withstanding, he is the most docile and gentle creature imaginable. The saddle horses are of the purest Canadian breed, very much resembling the horses which I saw in French Flanders. I presume they have originally come from that country. Every young man sports his riding horse here. There was a dinner at the Exchange after the Exhibition, and as a matter of course a good many got drunk and some little squabbling as in the old country. There were some Yankees in the company, the dislike to them was made manifest, and I feared would end in a row, as it is fully expected that America and Great Britain will have a brush—and they seem anxious to get at each other on this side of the Atlantic, but everything ended well.

Saturday 4 October. Was invited by Mr Thomson, the chairman of the Agricultural Association, to a ploughing match on his farm, which lies upon the banks of the Ottawa about 4 miles west of Bytown. Mr Lyon drove me out. This is the first farm which I have seen improved and enclosed with stone dykes and wrought after the same manner as at home. He has got an excellent stone house, completely furnished and as comfortable as any proprietors in the old country. A fine garden enclosed with stone and lime walls and all kinds of vegetables in abundance. He has about 12 acres of potatoes, the most luxuriant crop I ever saw. But he is some afraid of an early frost. Those farthest from the river appeared as if they had already got a nip. Those close upon rivers do not suffer so much as those inland, from frost. This, I think, is the reverse at home. I returned after taking some refreshment with Mr Lyon. Mr Thomson pressed me to stay dinner. There were 15 ploughs on the field, a goodly number for the backwoods of Canada. The ploughmen were making excellent work, but the field was of a light sandy nature and easily ploughed. Wages are high here. Mr Thomson gave his men £30 a year and found them. Remained at Mr Lyon's all night, spent the evening with Mr Sherriff, Mr Christie and some others.

Sunday 5 October. A wet day. Went to hear the Reverend Mr McKidds (Church of Scotland) in the forenoon and to the Episcopal Church[100] in the evening, along with Mr and Mrs Findlay, who had come up from Cumberland. Spent the evening with them.

Monday 6 October. Wrote George today telling him that I had received his letter of the 28th August upon the 23rd September and giving him an account of my sojourning in this country. There being horse racing in the vicinity of the town I went and saw them. They were well contested, and some very excellent races were run, but the ground was bad being merely a straight road leading into town—a good deal of betting— which caused, of course, some disputes, but all parties seemed to be wonderfully well up to the laws of the turf—but riding and horse racing are favourite amusements here, and greatly in vogue, down to the shop boy and lawyer's clerk, which account for the old country, Jocky-like manner everything was conducted. I left the race ground before the business was over, intending to sail in the evening by the Rideau Canal to Kingston upon Lake Ontario a distance of about 160 miles, but my friend Mr Richard Smith,[101] who had a steam boat concern upon the part of the River Ottawa called Lake Chaudière, invited me to accompany him to see the Chats Falls and Rapids, a distance of about 36 miles, and having intimated my design to Mr Thomas Keeffer,[102] government civil engineer to whom I had been previously introduced, he told me that he was just going to set out in the same direction and nearly 200 miles farther, and would be happy if I would accompany him the whole way.

7 UP THE OTTAWA RIVER AGAIN

Foot of Lake Chaudière

I at once accepted of his invitation and, without taking a single change of linen or stockings with me, set off with him and his brother by a stage coach over the worst road I had yet travelled since I had set my foot in Canada, and stopped at a place called Aylmer 9 miles from Bytown, the commencement of the navigation upon the Ottawa above Bytown. These 9 miles of the river are full of rapids, and can only be improved by a canal from the commencement of Lake Chaudière to a lock on the Rideau Canal. It being dark before we arrived I did not see the place. Waited upon Mr Blackburn,[103] the captain and half owner of the steamer to enquire after Mr Smith, who had taken another conveyance. I purchased stockings, nightcap and other articles at the captain's store, in some measure to prepare me for my long, and I was beginning to think, hazardous journey, which I understood had to be accomplished by sailing in an Indian bark canoe, and that we would have to look out for provisions and night quarters the best way we could as there were few settlers and no taverns on the route. Captain Blackburn very kindly invited me upstairs and introduced me to his wife and daughter—the latter is a very beautiful young woman. Mrs Blackburn is the sister of Sir James Campbell of Glasgow—Blackburn himself was unfortunate in business and emigrated with his family about twelve years ago. He is now doing well—after spending a few hours with the family I returned to the Inn—and went to bed.

Tuesday 7 October. Was roused this morning by half past five o'clock. Met with Mr Smith on board the steamer, started at six o'clock, arrived at the Chats Rapids about 12 o'clock. Had about 40 passengers on board. When I went to the steward

16 AYLMER, on the Ottawa River above Bytown. Muir reached here on 6 October by stagecoach from Bytown

to pay my passage money and bill of fare, he told me I had nothing to pay—the captain had given his orders—I, of course, thanked him kindly for this act of hospitality to a stranger, but he appears to be a kind, generous hearted fellow. We had now to leave him and Mr Smith and proceed through the Chats on our journey.

The Chats Falls and Rapids

I should like to give you some idea of this romantic place, before leaving it. We had already sailed about 36 miles upon what would in the old country be considered a pretty extensive lake, being about 8 miles broad. Upon approaching the falls we make a turn to the left around a headland when the lake or rather the river suddenly disappears before you, and forms itself, apparently, into an inland bay of about a mile long and half a mile broad. Here the stranger's attention is arrested. The most romantic scenery imaginable bursts upon his view all round this Bay—upon the one hand a romantic village (Fitzroy) perched upon the highland immediately above shews itself through gigantic trees, upon the other hand a cluster of islands, all covered with wood and so thickly dotted that they form a natural dam or breastwork and so completely confine the water, that it has to force its way through 32 different apertures or sluices forming as many beautiful waterfalls along the whole width of the river. Since a steam boat commenced running on Lake Chaudière many strangers visit these falls—but more on account of the number and the romantic scenery around than their magnitude. After travelling about two miles through these islands, until we passed the rapids, we again took the river and sailed for about two miles in a punt or large boat till we came to another steamer lying in deep water. This part of the river is called 'Lake des Chats' and is navigable by steam to a place called 'Portage du Fort'—a distance of about 30 miles from the Chats Falls. This Portage is the highest part of the Ottawa where steamers can go. In passing up we had to contend with several rapids and, before we were able to get through them, had to go into the eddies of these rapids, take off the steam and charge the valves with as much additional steam as possible, and then push through. This was somewhat dangerous not only

17   THE FALLS OF LES CHATS on the Ottawa River, reached by Muir on a steamer on 7 October. The falls were, he asserted, set in 'the most romantic scenery imaginable'

from an explosion of the boiler, but also from not getting over the rapids when we would have grounded and likely gone to pieces upon a sunk rock.

The Lake des Chats

However we all arrived safe a little after dark and put up at a comfortable hotel called the 'Portage'. The scenery has been very romantic today— innumerable islands in the lake as we pass along—few settlements to be seen.

Wednesday 8 October. I arose this morning in order to get a view of the place before starting—found it to be what I would say at home a 'romantic highland glen'. Came upon a piece of ground in a sequestered spot where I counted about 11 graves.[104] The ground was not enclosed, but some of the graves were enclosed with a wooden railing. The names of three individuals were inscribed upon a board at the head of their graves, which I took down being the first burial ground I had seen.
1 Ala Memoire de Jerime Febe ale mort le 15 de Feverie 1836— a le age de 22.
2 Sacred to the memory of Barnett McDonald who was drowned at the Mountain Boom on the 25 day of April 1836 aged 28 years.
3 Francis Bruneau.

Rapids of Portage du Fort

After breakfast Mr Keeffer his brother and I again set out upon our journey. The rapids extend about 8 miles, the first about 1 1/2 miles nearly to the Grand Calumet Island, which distance we walked on foot. After passing this rapid we sailed about 2 miles up the river till we came to another called Sauble Rapid, when we had again to walk till we passed the Grand Calumet Rapid. Here Mr Keeffer joined his surveying party and after having dined with Mr Nigle,[105] the overseer of the government work which is constructing for the conveyance of wood down river, we all set out in a bark Indian canoe, manned with six Irishmen in government pay as rowers or paddlers. The evening at first was beautiful, but I felt a little uneasy notwithstanding,

18 PORTAGE DES CHATS, one of the points on the Ottawa River at which canoes had to be carried round rapids

when we started off into the midst of what I considered a *mighty* river in so frail and so small a *bark*. There were now ten of us on board, which kept her down to the water's edge, and none durst move from the position he first placed himself; my legs began to cramp, and I was thinking how I should travel 300 miles in such a conveyance, when it began to rain, and Mr Keeffer proposed landing, which we soon did to my great satisfaction.

Grand Calumet

It being now dark and raining it was proposed that we should take up our quarters in a 'shanty' a short distance further on. Before we got there other three canoes had got ahead of us, and taken possession. We, however, after getting some supper squatted all around the room floor—we were, in all, about 40 in number of different nations, Indians, French Canadians, Scotch and Irish. Being somewhat fatigued I slept pretty soundly, but had off none of my clothes.

Thursday 9 October. Started this morning about six o'clock. Sailed up the river about 10 miles, landed, and the men cooked some breakfast at a shanty upon the riverside. Re-embarked and proceeded on our voyage till about one o'clock when we came to another shanty at the head of Grand Calumet River, or rather Lake, where we landed and dined.

Lake Allumettes

After our refreshment and resting for a little we again launched our canoe, but it rained heavy upon the lake, and night coming on we reached a shanty near the head of the lake upon an island called Des Allumettes where we got shelter during the night, but being drenched through and through I by no means felt comfortable in the idea of having to sleep upon a floor in wet clothes, my arm my only pillow and my wet plaid my covering! We only made out 25 miles today.

Friday 10 October. Got up this morning about 7 o'clock rather stiff and queerish, but I took a good horn of brandy and have felt nothing the worse. The island we left this morning I understand is about 24 miles long and 4 broad. There are 70 families upon it, all squatters, the island not being yet surveyed by the government. The number of inhabitants in whole are about 500 who live chiefly as lumberers. The Blue Mountains, or rather Hills, upon the north side of this lake, look beautiful at this season. The trees have assumed their autumnal hue and the variegated and inimitable rich colouring of the leaves of the different species of wood which are seen from the lake as rising gradually into two or three distinct tables form the most beautiful landscape in nature that could be imagined. I never saw anything resemble it in the old country. And when you look upon the face of the water the reflection of the variegated trees appears as from the brightest mirror, which heightens the beauty of the landscape in the greatest degree. This being a beautiful day, had every advantage of seeing this interesting and wild scenery. In the morning we proceeded about eight miles on our journey before breakfast. Soon after we came to the rapids called Kelbute, here we landed, and diverged for about a mile from the river, carrying our canoe and provisions upon our shoulders through a wild and narrow pass till we came again upon the lake.

Fort William Hudson Bay Post

After paddling for some time we crossed the lake and landed at a creek called Fort William,[106] the oldest post or station belonging to the Hudson's Bay Company upon the line of the Ottawa. A Mr McKenzie from Inverness[107] has charge at present. The company keep a store here for the accommodation of themselves and other travellers—Mr McK gave us some brandy and I purchased a bottle of rum. I saw a good many Indians, but Mr McKenzie says they are dying out fast. Fifty had died within a few years, which he attributed to bad living and taking too much spirits, which they are very fond of. After leaving Fort William we sailed to the mouth or entrance of the Deep River, and landed at a creek where we got some dinner prepared. The Deep River is a continuation of the Ottawa, but taking a westerly direction. A different name is given to this part of it which extends about thirty miles. We intended to remain all night at this creek, but the evening being beautiful and the moon full and the wind fair, we resolved to start and about six o'clock in the evening commenced our voyage. The wind continuing to blow pretty gently we set a small sail which I got charge of. In a canoe a sail is most dangerous, and requires constant, I may say momentary, attention, as the slightest extra puff of wind from a wrong quarter might upset the whole: being the most timid, and thereby likely to pay most attention, I was appointed to this post. Before ten o'clock we had run upwards of thirty miles almost without using a paddle. The moon being bright and full, and the steep banks, in some places nearly 1000 feet perpendicular, with the majestic Forest Trees hanging over the river, gave the scene a grand, wild and majestic appearance, and brought me nearer to Scotland than anything I have yet seen in America. But at the same time the idea of sailing in an Indian canoe at night upon a river in the wild and uninhabited parts of Canada, with I may say total strangers, produces feelings not easily to be described. We had now reached the rapid of the Deux Joachins, where we landed.

Rapids of the Deux Joachins.[108]

After landing we had considerable difficulty of getting under cover. The night was very cold, and there was no house within many miles of us excepting a house where a man resided who had married an Indian, but unfortunately for us we found the door padlocked and no person within. Having no other recourse and the night being so cold, we took off the lock, and entered the house—we raised a light and soon kindled a good fire, and prepared supper. There was a bed in the house, but we all squatted on the floor for the night keeping up a good fire. We had this day sailed about 50 miles, besides extra sailing amusing ourselves shooting at wild ducks which are very numerous. Mr Keeffer brought down one but did not kill it and so eager were our paddlers to get hold of it, that they actually pursued it for six miles down the river, without overtaking it, but I believe they would not have gone half the distance, had I not joked them and said I would tell when I went home that a lame duck had beat six Irishmen at a race. This fired their blood and had not Mr Keeffer insisted upon returning they would have seen the end of the chase one way or other. This gave them an additional pull of 12 miles.

Saturday 11 October. Joachins—I slept soundly last night; having got 'twixt a big Irishman and blazing fire, which was kept up all night and my plaid around me I was quite warm, but my head having fallen off my pillow (a block of wood) my neck was a little uneasy when I awoke. Two or three shakes made it all right, and after getting up and washed (I didn't require to dress) I was quite fresh. After breakfast Mr Keeffer informed me that he was going about two miles farther on to examine some government works called 'raft slides' which had given way, and that as this was his farthest destination, he intended to retrace his steps in the afternoon. His brother[109] and I went out with the gun, killed nothing. I also went and saw one of those 'slides'. They are a kind of pier erected on the river or by the side of it, of large logs or squared trees, and so constructed as to carry the rafts over the rapids. Many of the rapids upon the Ottawa formed a complete barrier to getting the large and valuable timber which grew upon its banks to market and to overcome this government has erected various 'slides' and 'sluices', and upholds them, for which a duty of 5/- currency is charged for every thousand feet of timber, which pass to Montreal. The duty levied upon the Ottawa for 1845 was £30,000.

19   TIMBER SLIDE AT LES CHATS

8 MEMORANDA RECORDING LETTERS POSTED

[These appear in the manuscript after the entry for events of 8 September] This letter to my boy put into the Post Office at Quebec on Wednesday the 10th of Sept. 1845. Alex Muir
To Master George F. Muir,
   Reverend George Tulloch
   Bellevue Academy
   By Aberdeen
   N.B.[110]

6 October. Wrote Geo. Muir from Bytown of this date, giving him a brief account of my journey from landing at Quebec to leaving this place (Sunday night).

Brockville, 18 October. Wrote George this date and put the *letter into the Post Office at Kingston.*

20 November Thursday. Port Dover. Wrote George of this date informing him of my journey, Indians etc., and that I thought I would winter in the States to give [word illegible] something of same date wrote Mr Ruxton.

23 November. Wrote Mr Grey of this date via Boston from Brampton.

NOTES

1   The barque *Lord Seaton* was built in 1840 and sailed regularly to North America under the command of William Talbot. She was of 300 tons, Old Measurement, or 440 tons, New Measurement, built mainly of hackmatack or larch, and had a male bust figurehead. Her builders at Kouchilbouguach, New Brunswick, were J. Cunard and Company, and her construction was supervised by William Rennie, who had earlier been engaged in shipbuilding at Aberdeen.

The vessel is an example of a phenomenon which by the 1840s was causing great concern to British shipbuilders—the invasion of their market by colonial built vessels. In March 1841 the *Lord Seaton* was advertised for sale at Aberdeen. Particulars of her were available from George Thompson, junior, pioneer of the Aberdeen Clipper Line, later to become provost of the town and her MP. Her purchasers were the said George Thompson, the skipper William Talbot, Neil Smith, junior (each having 8/64ths), and Henry Campbell Oswald and Charles George (40/64ths), of the firm Oswald, George, Insurance Brokers, which operated the vessel. By the end of April 1841 the *Lord Seaton* was registered *de novo* at Aberdeen. Her spring voyage that year was from Aberdeen back to her original port of registry, Miramichi, New Brunswick.

The *Lord Seaton* set sail from Aberdeen on 31 March 1845 for her spring voyage to North America. Circumstances surrounding the commencement of this voyage indicate an awareness by customs officials at Aberdeen of possible irregularities. Her skipper, Captain Talbot, had made no secret of the fact that her eventual destination was Quebec and that he was to pick up 'a full lading of passengers' in the north of Scotland. Aberdeen's Collector of Customs thought it politic to advise a member of his service at Cromarty that 'under the Passenger Act, he (Talbot) did not take on board here a sufficiency of bread stuffs'. After calling at Cromarty, where she remained on berth for a few days, she proceeded to Thurso, where she received emigrants as she lay in Scrabster Roads. She sailed from there on 16 April, and on 16 May she arrived at Quebec carrying seventy-two passengers (who enjoyed the presence of a surgeon on the voyage). She loaded up with timber and was cleared on 10 June at Quebec customs for the return crossing. By the third week in July her cargo was being unloaded at Aberdeen, where it was later sold by public roup.

On her second 1845 voyage to North America the *Lord Seaton* left Aberdeen on 3 August, as Muir reports. In his diary he mentions a few points of reference which allow the vessel's course to be traced to some extent. Two additional positions are known for her during the voyage: on 13 August she was spoken to by the *Douglas* in Lat. 53N, Long. 28W; on 19 August, she was spoken to in Lat. 48N, Long. 44W. Her arrival at Quebec on 9 September was first announced in Aberdeen in a newspaper of 4 October. At Quebec she again loaded up with timber, destined, according to one account, for Aberdeen, and to another, for Leven. Certainly she called at Cromarty early in November 1845. A report from there said

> This is the second voyage which has been completed by this fine vessel with emigrants from Scotland for Quebec this season, having on the first occasion, taken her departure from this place and Scrabster Roads in April. Captain Talbot reports having landed his passengers on both occasions in excellent spirits.

Another report could look forward to the future:

> ... the enterprising owners of this ship, Messrs Oswald, George, and Co., Aberdeen, intend in the ensuing spring to send her out again to North America with emigrants.

And so in early April 1846 the *Lord Seaton* again lay in Scrabster Roads to receive her emigrant passengers. Favourable comment was made on the quality and quantity of stores carried by the vessel—and Captain Talbot ordered bread. On Saturday, 11 April, the *Lord Seaton* set sail and 'was wafted away by the breezes to the American shores'. (*Aberdeen Directory*, 1842–3 and 1845–6; H M Customs, Aberdeen, Registers of Shipping for the Port of Aberdeen; *Aberdeen Herald*, 27 March, 17 April, 1, 4 May 1841, 21 June, 12, 19 July, 9 August, 22 November 1845; *Aberdeen Journal*, 9, 16 and 23 July, 13 August 1845; *Quebec Gazette*, 28 April, 17, 26 May, 11 June, 4 August, 17 September, 3 October 1845; *John O' Groat Journal*, 11 and 18 April, 14

November 1845; April 1846; Scottish Record Office, CE87/3/9, letter of 22 April 1841, and CE87/3/9, letter of 4 April 1845; Aberdeen Harbour, Sailings 1845, Arrivals 1845).

2   Muir's son, George.

3   The vessel was thus making about 100 miles a day—a rate she kept up until the end of her voyage of approximately 3,500 miles.

4   It is most unusual, perhaps even unique, to have a detailed breakdown, as given by Muir, of those on board a vessel sailing between the years 1830 and 1845 from Aberdeen to North America. The contemporary local newspapers sometimes mentioned the total number of passengers departing on a vessel. The government's emigrant agent at Quebec, Archibald Buchanan, does not, for individual vessels, give such full information as Muir.

The greatest number of passengers on one voyage, conveyed from Aberdeen to North America during the period 1830–45, could well have been that of the *Brilliant* on her 1832 spring voyage— 168. On 5 July 1842 the *Lord Seaton*, Talbot, arrived at Quebec from Sligo with 319 passengers: 107 males; 105 females; 107 children under 14. (*Aberdeen Journal*, Export List of March 1832; *House of Commons Sessional Papers*, 1843, (291) vol. xxxiv, in Buchanan's Report for 1842).

5   James Gordon and his brother Alexander (for whom see note 45) may have been the sons of Alexander Gordon and his wife Helen Gillespie (Old Machar parish, Aberdeenshire): they had sons with these names who were born in 1814 and 1823 respectively. James Gordon had resided in Aberdeen at 54 Summer Street, and at 72 Dee Street. He was employed as a traveller by the Aberdeen firm of Brebner and Ragg, general merchants, who were also described as tea merchants. Before he left Aberdeen for Quebec carrying with him 'the best wishes of a large circle of friends' James Gordon was entertained to a complimentary supper on Wednesday, 23 July 1845. The press account of the event reported: 'His frank and agreeable manners have gained for him universal esteem, and a stronger proof of the high opinion in which he is held could not be wished, than to see so many individuals meet to do him honour'. (*Aberdeen Directory*, 1842–3 to 1845–6; Aberdeenshire, parish of Old Machar, Old Parish Register; *Aberdeen Herald*, 26 July 1845; *Quebec Gazette*, 16 May 1845, 29 October 1845; J.B. Clearihue, *A Family Tree*, privately printed).

6   Muir gives a great amount of interesting information, so much

indeed that it becomes exasperating that he does not at times give more. Where was the cabin? How big was it? How was it furnished? It surely had more in it than a thermometer! And what did Muir have for dinner? What was 'on the menu' at other times? Who did the cooking and where were the meals served? Obviously, steerage passengers had made other arrangements, but Muir gives them, unfortunately, as little attention as his own. One of the most surprising omissions is any comment on the vessel's cargo. Not much is known about it from other sources, but she did carry 70,000 bricks, exported by A. and W. Nichol. Many loads of bricks were shipped from Aberdeen to British North America about this time. They were not just ballast, but no definitive explanation as to how they were used in Canada has yet been given in response to the editor's queries. House-building? Canal construction? For defence works on barracks? For the paving of streets? One James Johnston exported a clock and a horse. In view of Muir's background and the interest in farming which he later evinces in the diary it is surprising that the animal merits not even a mention. (*Aberdeen Journal* and *Aberdeen Herald*—Export Lists of various dates, 1830–45; *Aberdeen Journal*, 13 August 1845).

7 The Pentland Firth, fourteen miles across, lies between Caithness and the Orkney Islands. It is notable for the number and speed of its tidal currents, which make navigation difficult. Notwithstanding, it was the normal route taken by vessels bound for North America which had sailed from the east coast of Scotland or from the north east coast of England.

8 The vessel was indeed almost sixty years old. A brig of 312 tons, she was built in London in 1789, and traded mainly to Quebec and Miramichi in New Brunswick. Her skipper on this voyage was Captain McFarlane. She sailed from Alloa with a general cargo on 31 July 1845, and arrived at Quebec on 12 September. (*Lloyd's Register of British and Foreign Shipping*, 1844 and 1845; *Quebec Gazette*, 15 September 1845).

9 The Flannan Islands, which are also known as the Seven Hunters. They consist of seven small, uninhabited islands in Uig Parish, Lewis, twenty-one miles WNW of Gallon Head. In spite of the considerable danger they offered to shipping, it was not until the end of the nineteenth century that a lighthouse was erected there.

10 Just how the captain would have dealt with the situation had he found any stowaways would be worth knowing. Initiating a check on the fifth day out does not suggest that one of Talbot's

top priorities was their deposit on the shores of their native land. Persons stowing away aboard ships to North America had proved a sore problem to merchants in Aberdeen and other ports about ten years previously. Such clandestine emigration, as it was called, very often meant that a stowaway emigrant was leaving debt behind, that a merchant was being done out of his due. Merchants did not take kindly to their pockets being affected in this manner, and held meetings to organise methods of combatting the abuse. They proposed a tightening up of the law so that anyone intending to emigrate should publicly intimate the fact.

Circumstances surrounding the sailing from Aberdeen of the brig *Pursuit*, (Alexander Alexander master) on her spring 1834 voyage to Quebec gave rise to allegations of clandestine emigration—a person or persons had been smuggled aboard in casks of provisions. These allegations the brig's owner firmly denied. The incident caused a great furore in Aberdeen for a time, and gave rise to a press correspondence. (*Aberdeen Journal*, 28 August 1833, 7 May 1834, 15 April 1835, *Aberdeen Herald*, 26 April 1834, 10, 17, May 1834, 21 June, 2 August 1834).

11   *Botriphnie*. A mainly arable parish situated at the narrow 'neck' of Banffshire. It is bisected by the River Isla and its eastern boundary is contiguous with Aberdeenshire. Mid(dle) Third is in the valley of the Isla, about eight miles southwest of the town of Keith. 'Old Johnthan' is named in a later diary entry, of 9 September, as Sanders (Alexander) Mitchell. He has not been positively identified, but in the 1841 Census for the parish of Botriphnie an Alexander Mitchell (aged sixty-five) is mentioned as being at Mid Third. (*Census*, 1841, Banffshire, parish of Botriphnie).

12   An Aberdeenshire coastal parish, about twenty miles north of Aberdeen. One William Allardyce was residing in this parish in June 1841, at the farm of Ardendraught. He was aged fifty, and his wife Christian, was forty-five. They had four of a family. The Old Parish Register of Rathen (about twenty miles from Cruden) records that John Allardyce in Cairnbulg had a son by his wife Elisabeth Wylie baptised and called William on 21 December 1790. An entry for 10 January 1828 notes that 'William Allardyce and Christian Mitchell both in this parish were married'. Residing in Redhouse, they had three children baptised in the same parish. By 1835 the family had removed to Cruden, and on 5 February of that year 'William Allardice in Miltown of Ardendraught by his wife Christian Mitchell had a

son born and baptized upon the 11 said month named Joseph, witnesses Doctor Will and Miss Pratt'. The family does not appear in the 1851 Census for the parish of Cruden. They evidently had Episcopalian leanings, for the christenings of their children John and William are mentioned in Lonmay parish Episcopal records.

13   Eric Partridge in his *Dictionary of Slang* gives Jack Tar = a hornpipe.

14   Muir's Episcopal schoolmaster has been identified as William Logan, born to John Logan and his wife, Jean Keith, in the village of Longside, Aberdeenshire, on 6 May, 1823. It has been elsewhere stated that he studied at, and graduated from, Marischal College, Aberdeen, but this is not confirmed in P. J. Anderson's works. Emigration in 1845 was followed some five years later by his ordination by Bishop Bethune in Ontario. He served at Cartwright and Manvers, and at Fénélon Falls. He died at Toronto 11 April, 1896. (Parish of Longside, Aberdeenshire: Old Parish Register; Longside Parish, Aberdeenshire, *Census* of 1841; Information from Rev. R. M. Black, Trinity College, Toronto; *Canadian Churchman*, 23 April, 1896, 260; *Scottish Guardian*, xxvi, no 20, 316; *Scottish Notes and Queries*, Second Series, ii, 10).

15   In 1843 a split took place in the Established Church of Scotland—the Disruption. Many dissatisfied ministers and parishioners left the Established Church and set up the Free Church. The precentor, who led the praise, was a very important person in church worship in Scotland. An informative, and amusing, account of the precentor's role is to be found in Nicholas Dickson's *The Auld Scotch Precentor, as sketched in Anecdote and Story* (Glasgow 1894).

16   The total number of children has, for some reason, decreased by three from the figure of thirty-four Muir gives in his entry of Sunday 3 August.

17   Culsalmond is an Aberdeenshire parish, a mile or two south east of the small town of Huntly. Its population was mainly engaged in farming its sometimes not very hospitable acres, but in the 1840s some slate quarrying was still carried on in the parish. Perhaps the parish's sole claim to fame lies in a now largely forgotten episode, labelled in the exaggerated manner of the time 'the Culsalmond church riots' in the years immediately preceding the Disruption. The Rev. William Middleton was very much involved in the parish's troubles. He may, in 1845, have been carrying out his duties well in his instruction of

the girl who impressed Muir. At the beginning of the decade, however, the way he performed his duties was, not to put too fine a point on it, under scrutiny.

Middleton was educated at Marischal College, Aberdeen, and served as a military chaplain at Fort George, Inverness-shire. He came to Culsalmond in 1841 as assistant to the parish minister, the Rev. Ferdinand Ellis (died 1851). Age and other weaknesses were causing Ellis to neglect his duties in a manner quite unsatisfactory to his flock. The patron of Culsalmond church, Sir John Forbes, exercised his right to present Middleton as assistant and successor to Ellis. To this the majority of parishioners objected most strongly. Eighty-nine of the parish's one hundred and thirty-nine male heads of families, in their turn, exercised their right and dissented. The objection (which was to lead to the Disruption two years later) was to the appointment of ministers by lay patrons, but they claimed that they did not wish to accept a minister who, in their view, could be charged 'with the neglect of family worship, with attending to secular pursuits on the Lord's Day, with inattention to clerical duty, with carelessness in admitting persons to receive the sacraments, with cold unspiritual preaching'. The presbytery of Garioch, in whose jurisdiction Culsalmond lay, determined that Middleton should be settled. The settlement took place on 11 November 1841, amid doubt and confusion in and around the church and manse. A crowd of approximately two thousand was present, with the sheriff and police, to ensure that the law, both church and civil, was enforced. The question of Middleton's settlement went to a Commission of the General Assembly, which decided that he should meantime not officiate nor administer ordinances in the parish. The matter was pursued in the civil courts by Middleton, with the support of powerful backers. Action was taken against Dr Robertson, leader of the 'riotous' parishioners who objected to the settlement, but he was cleared of charges brought against him. Eventually things quietened down in Culsalmond and Middleton's settlement stood. He remained in the parish as minister until his death on 11 March 1853, aged seventy-three. (H. Scott, ed., *Fasti Ecclesiae Scoticanae*, vi, Edinburgh, 1926, 155; Robert Buchanan, *The Ten Years' Conflict, being the History of the Disruption of the Church of Scotland*, new edn., 1854, ii, chap.13; Alexander Smith, *A New History of Aberdeenshire*, Aberdeen, 1875).

18   Porpoises. The first written record of this expression noted by the *Scottish National Dictionary* is 1891.

19   See note 23.
20   The practice of throwing a bottle into the sea from a vessel somewhere on the vastness of the oceans was one which became common during the first half of the nineteenth century. It had a scientific purpose—gathering information on the strength and direction of currents. An early example of such a bottle was one put overboard from Captain Parry's *Hecla* in the Davis Straits on 16 June 1819. News of its recovery on Teneriffe, more than two years later, caused quite a stir. The *Nautical Magazine* provided a forum for news of bottles and in 1843 the magazine published a chart illustrating the course followed by bottles in the Atlantic. It was accompanied by a tabular list which detailed the bottles' history. (*Nautical Magazine*, 1843 etc.).
21   See note 66 below.
22   The *Heroine* was built at Dundee in 1831. She was ship-rigged, of 387 tons, and operated as a whaler for several years from that port. Early in 1838 ownership of her came into the hands of William Duthie, merchant, Aberdeen, and she became a familiar sight in Aberdeen's harbour as a regular trader between the port and North America, particularly Quebec. She offered excellent accommodation for cabin and steerage passengers. By 1845 a new, developing trade in guano was having an effect on many of Aberdeen's vessels, and it is not surprising to find that on 28 April 1845 the Heroine arrived at Aberdeen with 500 tons of guano from Ichaboe. She then set sail on 28 May from Aberdeen on a rather belated spring voyage to Quebec, with goods. She arrived there on 14 July, with goods and sixty-nine passengers. Having loaded up with timber, she cleared from Quebec on 6 August, and arrived at Aberdeen on 12 September. Her master on these 1845 voyages was Duncan Walker. Muir had a particular interest in the *Heroine*. He wrote from Quebec just after his arrival there to his brother-in-law, Alexander Findlay, reporting that 'I have heard nothing of my brother's family [i.e. George Muir's family, who were emigrating to Nichol Township] and Dr Stewart since they left Aberdeen. But we met the *Heroine*, the ship they went out in, on her homeward passage'. (H M Customs, Aberdeen, Registers of Shipping for the Port of Aberdeen; *Lloyd's Register of British and Foreign Shipping*; Aberdeen Harbour Records, Sailings and Arrivals, 1845; *Aberdeen Herald*, 3 July 1841; *Quebec Gazette*, 14 July, 6 August, 8 October 1845; Letter by Alexander Muir, printed in Appendix 1).
23   Pedestrian matches very often involving heavy wagers, enjoyed

a certain vogue among gentlemen in Britain during the last thirty years of the eighteenth century and into the nineteenth. At the turn of the century a Scots laird became quite practised in pedestrianism and noted for his feats. This was Captain Robert Barclay Allardice of Ury (1779–1854), near Stonehaven, and his exploits would have been known certainly to Muir, and perhaps to some of the others on the *Lord Seaton*. They excited such admiration and interest that Walter Thom, author of a *History of Aberdeen*, wrote a book entitled: *Pedestrianism; or An Account of the Performances of Celebrated Pedestrians during the Last and Present Century; with a full Narrative of Captain Barclay's Public and Private Matches; and An Essay on Training* (Aberdeen, 1813). Shortly before the *Lord Seaton* sailed from Aberdeen two pedestrian events were held on the town's links. On 5 July 1845, an Irishman, M'Mullin, walked sixty miles in under twelve hours. The following Saturday he performed again at the same location, thirty miles in less than six hours—half the distance being covered walking backwards! (*Aberdeen Herald*, 12, 19 July, 1845).

24   Henry Wolsey Bayfield retired from active service in the Royal Navy with the rank of Captain in 1856. He was born at Kingston upon Hull, England, on 21 January 1795 and died at Charlottetown, Prince Edward Island, on 10 February 1885. He entered the Royal Navy as a boy and served on various Atlantic stations and in the American War of 1812. After the latter he was engaged in surveying the Great Lakes. His good work there led to his being put in charge of surveying operations in the River St Lawrence, the Gulf and its approaches, which became his life's work. His surveys were to make this notoriously dangerous area much safer for the increasing amount of shipping it was to carry. Bayfield kept good records of his work and his *Survey Journals, 1829–53*, have recently been edited, with an introduction, by Ruth McKenzie, and issued by the Champlain Society (Toronto, 1984–6). In the course of his career Bayfield also contributed various articles on the St Lawrence to the *Nautical Magazine*. Muir, as he admits, leans heavily on Bayfield for his Anticosti information. It looks as if Captain Talbot might have given him access to a work prepared by Bayfield— *Sailing Directions for the Gulf and River of St Lawrence*, (Admiralty Hydrographic Office, London, 1837). (*Dictionary of Canadian Biography*, vol.xi; Boase, *Modern Biography*; W.R. O'Byrne, *A Naval Biographical Dictionary*, London, 1849).

25   The wreck of the *Granicus* and its aftermath, once news of it

broke, had shocked the outside world: survivors had indulged in cannibalism. In his *Survey Journals*, 3 August, 1829, Bayfield gives a fuller account of 'the most horrible misery' to which Muir alludes. Muir reports seeing 'a large ship on shore upon the Island of Anticosti': two vessels are known to have been on shore on the Island about this time—the *Osprey* of Leith and the *Dumfriesshire*. (Bayfield *Survey Journals*; *Times*, 18 July, 24 September 1829; *Quebec Gazette*, 10 and 15 September 1845).

26   The *William Dawson*, 481 tons, was a ship-rigged vessel, built at Lancaster in 1812. She sailed regularly to North America from ports on the Forth. On this voyage she set sail from Alloa on 2 August 1845, and arrived at Quebec on 8 September, her skipper being Captain Beveridge. There were four passengers: the Rev. Mr Aitken, Mr James Watt, Miss Watt and Miss Agnes Watt. (*Lloyd's Register of British and Foreign Shipping*, 1844 and 1845; *Quebec Gazette*, 8 September, 10 September 1845).

27   Bayfield terms it Pointe de Mille-Vaches and the area is designated Portneuf by Joseph Bouchette on his map. It is on the north shore of the St Lawrence, a few miles downstream from where the River Saguenay flows into it. (Bayfield, *Survey Journals*; J. Bouchette, *A Topographical Dictionary of the Province of Lower Canada*, London 1832).

28   Captain David M. Rae had been one of the promising young shipmasters produced by the port of Aberdeen. After his apprenticeship, he served as an officer on the East Indiaman, *Barrossa*. He became First Officer of the *Aberdeenshire*, Captain Martin, a regular trader between Aberdeen and Halifax, and this prepared him well for gaining his first command in or about 1835. This was the brig *Amity*, 311 tons, built in New Brunswick in 1825. By the time Rae became associated with her the vessel was registered in Aberdeen and her two main owners were the brothers John and William Gray, fishcurer and horse-hirer respectively. Rae owned eight sixty-fourths. As her skipper he did at least three round trips between Aberdeen and Quebec in 1835–6. By the following year he was captain of the barque *Cyrus*, 400 tons, which sailed regularly between London and Quebec. It is the wreck of this vessel to which Muir refers. The *Aberdeen Journal*, in its issue of 1 January 1845, reported that it had gleaned particulars of the event from various authentic sources:

About the beginning of November (1844), a severe gale of wind not only did much damage along the American coast, but was also severely felt in the Atlantic, as we have learned from some vessels that have since arrived. After leaving Quebec, the *Cyrus* was overtaken by the gale accompanied with snow, and went ashore on Point Neuf, and struck so heavily that the mainmast went through her. The crew took to the rigging, where they struggled with snow, wind, and sea, for thirty-two hours, which they were enabled to surmount with the exception of two. They were at last taken ashore by the Indians, and ultimately reached Quebec. The Captain, in such circumstances, is always the last to leave the deck, and Mr Rae, accordingly, when the crew took to the rigging, occupied a position near the companion-door; but the boats having been dashed to pieces, the decks torn asunder, and the companions swept away, the Captain, in attempting to take the rigging, was dashed on deck by a heavy sea, and then swept overboard. Thus perished this meritorious seaman at the early age of 32 years, leaving a wife and child to lament his loss; but she shares the sympathy of the numerous circle of friends in which her husband was known and esteemed.

(Angus and Mearns Burgh Register and Almanac for 1836; Lloyd's Registers; H M Customs, Aberdeen, Registers of shipping for the Port of Aberdeen; Aberdeen Harbour Board Records, Sailings and Arrivals 1835 and 1836).

29 Green Island was a hazard to navigation and had a lighthouse on it. It lies almost immediately opposite the mouth of the Saguenay.

30 Red Island, six miles north of Green Island. It also had a lighthouse.

31 Muir has written Lerwick instead of Limerick. In his report for the year 1841 A.C. Buchanan, government emigration agent at Quebec, twice mentions the wreck on Red Island of the barque *Minstrel*, 296 tons, Captain Outerbridge, from Limerick. She had set sail on 21 April with 140 passengers. Buchanan gives two dates for the wreck—8 and 18 May, 1841. Only four of the passengers and four of the crew of fifteen were saved. They completed their voyage to Quebec on the vessel *Wellington*, Captain M'Intire. The *Quebec Gazette* gave a list of passengers and crew.(*House of Commons Sessional Papers*, 1842, [373], xxxi, Correspondence Relative to Emigration, Despatch from the Governor General of British North America, Transmitting the Annual Reports of the Agents for Emigration in Canada, 1841, pages 5 and 14 of Buchanan's Report; *Quebec Gazette*, 24 May 1841).

32 The *Brilliant* was the best known of Aberdeen's regular traders with British North America, though she also made voyages to

New York. On occasion she left Aberdeen with more than one hundred emigrants. Aberdeen built in 1814, of 332 tons, she had a long connection with the Aberdeen shipping family of Duthie. Alexander Duthie was her master when she left Aberdeen 3 April 1835, for New York. Some of her 108 passengers were to provide 'reinforcements' for the settlements such as Bonaccord which had recently been established, largely by folk from Scotland's eastern counties north of the Tay, in Nichol Township.

The *Brilliant*, Captain James Elliott, stuck, during fog, on Red Island, while on her spring voyage of 1838. The steamboat *British America* towed her up to Quebec, where she arrived 'in a very leaky condition' on 12 May. Repairs were carried out on her after she had been put on the slip at Pointe Levy, and she was cleared at Quebec for Aberdeen on 28 June. (J. Connon, *Elora, the Early History of Elora and Vicinity*; *Aberdeen Journal*, 8 April 1835; *Aberdeen Herald*, 16 June 1838; *Quebec Gazette*, 14, 28 May, 29 June 1838; Aberdeen Harbour Records, Sailings 1835 and 1838).

33   The *Rob Roy* was a brig of 241 tons, registered at Aberdeen and owned by the firm of Catto and Company of that port. She is an example of Aberdeen's involvement in the emigration trade between Ireland and North America as early as the mid 1820s. Her 1827 voyage, with W. Kenn as skipper, from Belfast to Quebec was her last. The wreck of the *Rob Roy* took place late in April or early May 1827. It was a period of very stormy weather in the Gulf and River St Lawrence, and during it the *Rob Roy* was driven on to the south shore of the river, in the County of Lislet, probably close to the telegraph station of the same name. Muir exaggerates in his retelling of the event; a newspaper account reports that 'about 25 of the passengers drowned'. Two other Aberdeen vessels suffered during the same bout of stormy weather in the St Lawrence—the *City of Aberdeen*, Duthie, and the *Brilliant*, Barclay, both lost anchors and cables. (*Lloyd's Register of Shipping*, 1825–6 to 1828–9; *House of Commons Sessional Papers*, 1836 (in 567), xvii, Return of All Ships Registers Cancelled or Given Up on Account of the Loss or Destruction of the Ships. ... Appendix No 8 of Report from Select Committee on Shipwrecks, 340; Bouchette, *Topographical Dictionary of the Province of Lower Canada*; *Aberdeen Journal*, 13 June 1827).

34   The Quarantine Station was set up by the authorities in an attempt to prevent immigrants from bringing the dreaded cholera into the Canadas. For many of the immigrants their experi-

ence of the New World was to end here in a mass grave. The
island of Grosse Ile, on which the station was sited, belies its
name, being only 1,300 hectares or so in area. In his *Survey
Journal* Captain Bayfield reports in the entry of Friday, 27 April
1832: '... Dr Griffin, Captn Alderson, R.E., went down to Grosse
Ile to make arrangements for the Quarantine establishment on
that Island'. Within a month Captain James Anderson of the
Aberdeen vessel *Quebec Packet*, with nine passengers, discovered
that Quarantine Regulations had to be obeyed—he was fined
£10 by the (Quebec) Board of Health for not anchoring his
vessel at the mouth of the River St Charles. (Bayfield *Survey
Journals*, i, 165; T. Dukes, 'La Grosse Ile and its Memorials', in
Families, 26, 1987, 201–212; *Quebec Gazette*, 25 May 1832).

35   The 'Irishman' could well have been the *Governor*, 307 tons,
Captain D. Gorman(d), of Limerick. She sailed from that port
on 1 August 1845, and arrived at Quebec on 9 September with
110 passengers. (*Lloyd's Register of Shipping*; *Quebec Gazette*, 8, 10,
12 September 1845).

36   This was a very favourable length of crossing: times varied
enormously. In 1842 the average length of crossing of vessels
arriving at Quebec from ports in Great Britain and Ireland was
forty-six days. The vessels which arrived at Quebec during the
week 13 August to 20 August 1842, took on average for the
crossing fifty-seven days. Between March and August 1843 the
shortest passage to Quebec took twenty-seven days, and the
longest, eighty-eight days. It was a source of satisfaction to a
skipper and his vessel's owner/agent were she the first of the
new season's arrivals at Quebec from Britain. Aberdeen vessels
gained such distinction on three occasions between 1813 and
1831: the brig, *Patriot*, Anderson, arrived at Quebec on 7 May
1818, after a voyage of thirty-eight days from Aberdeen; the
same vessel and skipper accomplished a similar feat in the following year, arriving at Quebec on 1 May after a crossing of
thirty-five days; the brig, *Quebec Packet*, Anderson, was the first
arrival at Quebec in 1827, on 30 April, taking only twenty-
eight days for the crossing. The port of Quebec was open for
approximately six months in the year—May to November,
depending on the ice in the St Lawrence—and it was usual for
vessels to do two round trips across the Atlantic per season. The
first vessel to make three round trips was the *Sophia*, Captain
Neil. This was done in the 1831 season, and in the following
year Quebec admirers presented him with a silver cup to com-
memorate his achievement. (A.C. Buchanan, Government

Agent at Quebec, Yearly Reports 1832–47, in *Parliamentary Papers*; *Quebec Gazette*, 2 May 1832, 24 October 1831, 19 October 1832).

37   Alexander Findlay was Alexander Muir's brother-in-law, having married Margaret Muir on 28 January 1826 in the parish of Slains, Aberdeenshire. The evidence suggests that he belonged to the neighbouring parish of Cruden and had an attachment to the Episcopalian Church there (the Muir family was Presbyterian). He was most probably the Alexander Findlay baptised in Nook, Cruden, on 12 October 1793, the son of Alexander Findlay and Jean Ironside. An Alexander Findlay in Little Mains, Cruden, was confirmed 17 July 1811, by the Episcopalian clergyman, the Right Reverend John Skinner.

For about the first eight years of their marriage Alexander Findlay and his wife, Margaret, resided in Cruden, at Little Mains of Auchleuchries. The precise date of their emigration to British North America is not known. Alexander, while at Auchleuchries, received, possibly in 1833 or 1834, from William Duthie, Aberdeen, details of fares from Aberdeen to Quebec: cabin with provisions £10; steerage passage without provisions £2.15.0; steerage passage with provisions £5. They settled in the Ottawa Valley, in the Township of Lochaber, on Lot 27, Concession 1. By 1842 the family had moved slightly upstream, and over to the opposite shore, to the Township of Cumberland, to Gore Letter E, Concessions 7 and 8, New Survey. It was here that Alexander Muir found them.

Five children are known to have been born to the Findlays in Cruden: Mary, 31 October 1827; Jane Muir, 24 December 1829; twin sons, Alexander and John, 2 November 1831; and George, 1 February 1834. A son, William, was born at Lochaber in September 1836. It is strange that only one child should be mentioned by Muir in the diary, and stranger still, perhaps, that she is not referred to by name.

Alexander Findlay and his son, George were drowned in the Ottawa, near Taylor's Farm, in the late autumn of 1846, while returning from Bytown with winter supplies. In the period immediately following the catastrophe, helped by relatives in the homeland, the family managed to keep their Cumberland holding. Margaret Findlay, née Muir, died in November 1874.

When Alexander Findlay and his wife had come out to Lochaber they had left their twin boys behind in Aberdeenshire. They came out to their parents' Cumberland home in 1842, in the brig *Gem*. She was advertised when lying at Leith—'198

tons per register, Peter Robb, Commander ... (with) first rate
accommodation for Cabin as well as a limited number of steerage passengers'. The vessel did not depart from Leith on the
date originally intended, 10 June— not an unusual occurence
with vessels to North America. A later advertisement described
her as 'a most desirable conveyance', having 'still room for 3
Cabin and 28 steerage passengers'. The *Gem* was an Aberdeen
vessel, and on this delayed voyage called there on 27 June. She
left Aberdeen on 28 June for, harbour records say, New York.
There was, therefore, opportunity for the Findlay twins to join
the brig at Aberdeen, rather than Leith. The *Gem* is specifically
mentioned in the Weekly Report Section of Quebec Emigrant
Agent Buchanan's Report for 1842. She arrived at Quebec 24
August 1842, a date which lends credence to New York being
a previous port of call. From Quebec she went upstream to
Montreal, where it is most likely the twins disembarked. Buchanan mentions that the vessel—from Leith, no mention of Aberdeen or New York— carried as passengers, 16 males, 7 females,
and 7 children under the age of 14. They were described as
'mechanics, labourers, and one farmer'. It is a fair assumption
that this one farmer was the person in whose charge the twins
were travelling, their uncle, George Muir. He delivered the boys
to the Findlay homestead and then proceeded west to review
prospects for himself and his own family. (Upper Canada Land
Index, Films 105 and 108; various documents from the Land
Registry Office, Russell, Ontario, for Cumberland Township;
various maps of Cumberland Township, particularly the 1862
map of the Counties of Stormont, Dundas, Glengarry, Prescott
and Russell, Canada West, surveyed H.F. Walling; Lloyd's
Register of British and Foreign Shipping, 1837–45; *The Scotsman*,
8, 11 June 1842; *Aberdeen Herald*, 4 June 1842; Aberdeen Harbour Records, Sailings, 1842; Old Parish Registers, Parishes of
Slains and Cruden, Aberdeenshire; Register of Baptisms, 1807–
60, St James' (Episcopal) Chapel, Cruden, Aberdeenshire;
Dale's Cemetery Inscriptions, Cumberland Township, Ontario;
House of Commons Sessional Papers, 1843, (291), vol. xxxiv, in
the Weekly Returns of Buchanan's Report for 1842; private
information from Findlay family descendants).

38   Elora lies fourteen miles north west of Guelph in southern Ontario. Alexander Muir's eldest brother, George (1784–1855), in
the 1841 census, parish of Slains, Aberdeenshire, is recorded
farming at Nether Leask, with his wife, Jean (née Wilken) and
their eight children. He lost the lease of Nether Leask shortly

afterwards. He became acquainted with Nichol Township, Wellington County, Ontario, and prospects there in 1842, and by 1845 he and his family had settled on Lot 4, Concession 15. Lot 5 also became Muir family property. Nichol Township, in the years around George Muir's arrival, was a common area of settlement for families from North East Scotland. Many were attracted to settlements largely established under the aegis of Adam Fergusson of Woodhill, Perthshire, and James Webster of Balruddery, Angus. Cadenhead, Dingwall-Fordyce, Emslie, Fasken, Gerrie, Michie, Mair, Tytler, are only some of the names of families from the North East of Scotland who made their homes in this area. They took North East names with them, such as Aboyne and Bonaccord: George Muir gave his homestead a very Aberdeenshire-sounding name—Nethermuir.

No record survives of Alexander Muir's visit to Nichol Township and his brother, George. The notes which immediately precede the Diary entry of Tuesday, 9 September 1849, suggest that it took place right after his time in the Bytown area, and that it was over and done with by 20 November, when he was at Port Dover. (*Aberdeen Journal*, 23 January 1856; A.D. Fordyce, *Family Record of the Name of Dingwall-Fordyce in Aberdeenshire*, Fergus, Ontario, 1888; D.M. Beattie, *Pillars and Patches Along the Pathway. A History of Nichol Township*, Nichol, 1984; *Census*, 1841, Aberdeenshire, parish of Slains; Private information from Muir and Findlay families descendants).

39 See note 11 above.

40 The notice praising Captain Talbot and his vessel appeared in the *Quebec Gazette* of 10 September 1845:

> The *Lord Seaton*, Captain Talbot, of and from Aberdeen, arrived here last night with 64 passengers, after a voyage of 36 days all well.
>
> The whole passengers on board the *Lord Seaton*, having experienced the greatest kindness and attention from Captain Talbot, during their passage from Aberdeen, feel it their duty to make this public acknowledgment of the same, by recommending him to their friends and countrymen, who may be intending to emigrate to America, as a person of much kindness and every way qualified to render all on board comfortable. The *Lord Seaton* is a commodious, fast-sailing and seaworthy Barque,
>
> Quebec, 9th September, 1845.

Aberdeen newspapers published items with a similar message, submitted at times, no doubt, in the hope of a bit of free advertising. Praising captain, crew and vessel as they did, they also allayed to a degree the fears of likely voyagers.

41 On 13 September 1759 a British army under General James Wolfe scaled a cliff under cover of darkness and defeated a French army under the Marquis de Montcalm on the Plains of Abraham. Both generals were mortally wounded. The battle was decisive for the future of Canada, and four years later the Treaty of Paris ceded 'New France' to Britain.

42 During the American War of Independence the Americans captured Montreal and laid siege to Quebec. But their attack on the town on 31 December 1775, led by Richard Montgomery and Benedict Arnold, was a failure. Montgomery was killed, Arnold wounded.

43 A calèche was a two-wheeled horse-drawn carriage, usually open, once popular in French Canada.

44 The first of the two fires which devastated Quebec (which was composed largely of wooden buildings) in 1845, took place on 28 May, starting in a tannery at the foot of Abraham's Hill on the road leading to Scott's Bridge. Fanned by a strong gale from the west, flames quickly spread and streets were engulfed. The District Military Commander, whose troops by their fire-fighting exertions prevented an even bigger calamity, estimated that about 1,500 homes had been burned—a figure which proved to be an under-estimate. At least a score of lives were lost. The suburbs of St Roch's were the areas which suffered most. The second fire broke out on the night of 28 June and seemed more terrifying than the first, a gale from the east making fire-fighting more difficult. Large areas of St John's suburbs were destroyed on this occasion. Committees and subscription lists were set up in the United Kingdom and possessions to help provide relief for Quebec and its inhabitants, whose hopes were well expressed by 'A Citizen' in a letter to the *Quebec Gazette* of 30 May: he hoped that 'London and all the other leading commercial cities in the United Kingdom' would 'come to our assistance in this, the greatest calamity that ever befel a City in a British Colony'. On receipt of a letter from the Mayor of Quebec, Aberdeen Town Council 'agreed to cause subscription papers be placed in the banks and other public offices of the city and to commence the subscription themselves as individuals'. But at the end of a few weeks the *Aberdeen Herald* had to comment: 'The amount of private subscriptions from Aberdeen, we are sorry to say, is hitherto quite unworthy of the city'. Therefore when Aberdeen Town Council met on 18 August 1845 and 'the small amount

subscribed out of doors' was 'strongly animadverted on, several members of the Council agreed to increase their subscriptions, and it was also agreed to give £10 from the City Treasury'. (British Parliamentary Papers, House of Lords, (41) 1847, Correspondence Relating to the Conflagrations at St John's and Quebec; *Quebec Gazette*, 30 May, 2 June 1845; *Aberdeen Herald*, 23 August 1845; Aberdeen Town Council Minutes, vol. 77, Nov. 1843—Nov. 1846, pp.124 and 130—Meetings of 14 July and 18 August 1845).

45 Neither the date of Alexander's leaving Aberdeen for Quebec (possibly on the *Brilliant's* spring voyage of 1841) nor the reason for his going is known. In Quebec he operated mainly as a merchant. In the spring of 1845 he was offering for sale 'British Plate Glass' and also 'an assortment of superior English leather, consisting of Cordovan, Calf Skin, Wax Kip Butts, Harness Hides'. All these could be obtained from his premises at 25 St Peter Street, Quebec. An A. Gordon in Quebec was the agent for the *Lord Seaton* on her spring 1845 voyage. In October of that year an Alex. Gordon in Quebec advertised that he was wanting to charter 'a vessel of about 400 tons to load square timber for the East Coast of Scotland'. Alexander Gordon was married on 8 May 1844 in Quebec, by the Rev. Dr Cook, to Eleanor, daughter of James Clearihue. In the Quebec Census, taken 11 January 1852, Alexander Gordon's age is given as thirty-three, and his birthplace as Aberdeen. His wife's age was thirty, and her birthplace Quebec. Their family comprised five girls, the eldest aged seven, and the youngest aged one year. He is designated as a merchant—obviously of some substance, as there were four female servants in the household.

46 In some ways Mr Clearihue is a bit of a mystery. In others, he can be pinpointed. With the help of Muir's remarks we can conclude that he is James Clearihue (the surname is variously spelt), who had a successful bakery establishment in St Vallier Street, Quebec City. Some of his wealth went into the farm (Lot 279) in nearby Charlesburgh, on the River St Charles. For that reason, perhaps, he supported the plan of a canal being formed in the River St Charles to ensure navigation at all times. He had a certain standing in the community as a Justice of the Peace, a member of Quebec City Council, and a manager of Quebec St Andrew's Society. He was a loyal subject of the Crown: his signature appears in the Quebec citizens' Loyal Address presented to Lord Dalhousie in 1827, and he was among those who petitioned for a public meeting, which would draw up

an address of congratulations to His Excellency the Governor-General on the latter's arrival in Quebec in 1841.

Operating a bakery in a cramped quarter of Quebec had its particular danger. Mr Clearihue's stables were burned down in October 1843, and the conflagrations of 1845 caused even greater havoc to his property. Coping with the latter emergency —which eventually entailed making use of the Commissariot Bakery—was obviously too much for Mr Clearihue. He gave the business over to his son, also named James. James Clearihue senior did not long survive the upheaval of the fires. A summer visit to the spa of Caledonia Springs in 1846 had no great beneficial effect, and he died on 7 March 1847. His widow Anne, née Badenoch, lived on in comfortable circumstances until 1888.

James Clearihue senior had a daughter, Eleanor, who, as we have seen, became the wife of Alexander Gordon. Her brother, James Clearihue junior, born about 1818 in Quebec, continued the bakery business, but a spirit of adventure rather than of business acumen seems to have gained the upper hand in his life. The business, by now Clearihue and Frew, collapsed about 1860. James Clearihue junior went to Australia some years later in pursuit of gold, where, it is believed, he died. He had married Miss Mary Vass in Montreal on 4 June 1839. It is believed that he later married for a second time. Descendants are today to be found in British Columbia and in California. It is likely that a John Clearihue, died 1835; Ann Hobbs, née Clearihue, died 1844 at the age of 54; and James Clearihue senior, died 1847— all deaths occurring in Quebec—were members of the family of Peter Clerihew (sic) and his wife Elspet/Margaret Gordon, in the parish of Midmar, Aberdeenshire. (J.B. Clearihue, *A Family Tree*, privately printed; *Quebec Gazette*, 21 August, 18 September 1835, 7 June 1839, 19 May, 22 October 1841, 20 May, 7, 30 November, 2 December 1842, 6, 9 October, 22 November 1843, 10 May, 9, 18 October 1844, 30 May, 2, 6 June, 7 July, 3, 8, 10 September 1845; National Archives of Canada, Lower Canada Marriage Bonds, Microfilm H-1130, Item No. 921; National Archives of Canada, Censuses of 1851 and 1861, Canada East, Quebec City, St Peter's Ward, Valier Street; Quebec City Census, 1851, Palace ward).

47   A more vivid account of such a floating island, given by another North East Scot, James Thomson, is quoted by Arthur R.M. Lower, *Great Britain's Woodyard*, Montreal, 1973, 204. On 7 June 1844 Thomson wrote to his father, Alexander Thomson,

Aboyne, Aberdeenshire

> We had not gone far up the river from Quebec City when we saw some more wonders ... an immense field of floating timber, the logs squared and built upon one another—I don't know how deep—there were a dozen masts upon it with a sail on each, a great many men with wooden houses and fires and the whole pulled along by a steamer. The first one was scarcely passed when we saw another.

48   Mentioned in R.W. MacKay, *Montreal Directory for 1842–3* and Stephen Leacock, *Leacock's Montreal*, ed. J. Culliton (revised edn., Toronto, 1963).

49   Peter Nicol was the son of Peter Nicol, a merchant in Old Aberdeen, and his wife Ann Jaffray. The reason for the presence of Peter in Montreal is not known. See note 56.

50   George Auldjo (1790–1848), a son of George Auldjo of Portlethen. An Aberdeen merchant who was provost of Aberdeen 1791–2, the elder George was bankrupt by 1799. He died in 1806. The younger George was educated at Aberdeen Grammar School, and by 1816 was working in the Montreal firm of Maitland, Garden and Auldjo—the 'Auldjo' having been his uncle Alexander (1758–1821). A prominent citizen of Montreal, his life had not been without adventure. In 1831 he and his daughter Jane were saved from the wreck of the *Sherbrooke* off Cape Breton, and in 1840 he was aboard the *Sir Robert Peel* at Wellesley Island, New York, when she was attacked by Upper Canada Patriots: he was robbed of £600. (*Dictionary of Canadian Biography*, vol. vii; J.M. Bulloch, 'The Family of Auldjo', in *Scottish Notes and Queries*, xii, no.8, Third Series, August 1934, 113–19; W. McBean, *Biographical Register of the St Andrew's Society of New York*, vol. i, New York, 1922; A.R. Newsome, ed., 'Records of Emigrants from England and Scotland to North Caroline, 1774–1775', in *North Carolina Historical Review*, 11 (1934); T. Watt, *Aberdeen Grammar School, Roll of Pupils, 1795–1919, annotated from 1863*, Aberdeen, 1923; *London, England, Directories, 1790–1826*; N. Bosworth, ed., *Early Days of Montreal*, Montreal, 1839, 138; *The Auldjo Papers, Introduction and Listing*, Queen's University, Kingston, Ontario, November, 1981; Old Parish Register, parish of St Nicholas, Aberdeen, Aberdeenshire; *Aberdeen Ceramics*, Aberdeen Art Gallery, 1981, 8–16; *Quebec Gazette*, 22 August 1831, 9 November, 1832, 5 July 1834, 26 May 1837).

51   James Jamieson, Licentiate of the Royal College of Surgeons of

Edinburgh, MD of Marischal College, Aberdeen. He married Anna Maria, the fifth of the younger George Auldjo's six sisters. (P.J. Anderson, ed., *Fasti Academiae Mariscallanae Aberdonensis, 1593–1860*, ii, New Spalding Club, 1898; J.M. Bulloch, 'The Family of Auldjo', in *Scottish Notes and Queries*, xii, 8, Third Series, August 1934, 113–19).

52   Writing during World War II, Stephen Leacock said of Rasco's Hotel that it 'is still standing today, ignominiously crowded out by a market, battered, dingy, its ornamentation gone, its garment divided, its very lettering fallen in part away, with nothing but the recollection of Charles Dickens' visit there in 1842 to keep a faint breath of survival stirring'. Rasco arrived in Montreal from Italy in 1819. After trying his hand at various occupations he took ownership of an inn on Capital Street, which he dubbed The Belfast Hotel. He then became associated with the running of The British-American Hotel, and when it was burned down in April, 1833, he decided to build his own establishment, 'the most splendid hotel of the age, for fifteen years the center of life in Canada'. Rasco's Hotel was completed in 1836 and was still under the Italian's control when Muir visited it in 1845. One might have expected Muir to have written more about the hotel, but perhaps the Bill of Fare had overawed him. (A.V. Spada, *Les Italiens au Canada*, Canada Ethnica VI, Ottawa, 1969).

53   A very full description of the cathedral is given in J. Bouchette, *The British Dominions in North America* (London, 1832), i, 217–22.

54   This was the Reverend William Arnot, 1808–75. He was licensed by the presbytery of Glasgow in 1837, and began his ministry in St Peter's, Oswald Street, Glasgow in 1839. He and his congregation 'came out' in the Disruption, he having been one of the ministers who signed the Act of Separation and the Deed of Demission. He became minister of the Free High Church, Edinburgh, in 1863, and remained there until his death.

The early Free Church was anxious to sustain its brethren overseas and Arnot was one of the ministers invited by the Free Church Commission in Edinburgh to go to North America to give encouragement to the young church. He set sail on his first trip to that continent in May 1845 from Liverpool, in the *Britannia*. Later he was to decline the opportunity of a charge in Canada.

During this first trip he kept regularly in touch with his St Peter's Congregation. On Monday, 25 June he wrote to them

It has been so ordered that the greater part of my travelling in Canada has been accomplished during the first month. I have been five Sabbaths in the country. Two of these have been spent in Montreal, one in the Lower province in certain villages and two in the Upper province—Toronto and Coburg. Almost the whole of my time now will be devoted to Montreal.

One of the two Montreal Sabbaths was the 1 June 1845, when he preached at eleven o'clock am and seven o'clock pm, in the New Free Church, Côté Street.

On Monday, 14 July 1845 the *Montreal Gazette* carried the following notice

We are requested to intimate that by request, the Rev. Mr Arnold of Glasgow will deliver an address to the Associated Sabbath School Teaching of this city this evening (Monday) in the New Free Church, head of Côté St at 8 o'clock precisely. All Teachers and others interested in Sabbath School instruction are respectfully invited to attend.

Arnot can be traced preaching in Quebec in September 1845.

In view of Muir's experience of Roman Catholicism in Montreal it is interesting to note what Mr Arnot thought about 'Popery' in Canada. After barely a week in Lower Canada, he wrote home to his Free St Peter's congregation on 28 May 1845

You are aware that Lower Canada is a popish country. I have seen Popery more triumphant and less disguised here than ever I saw it in Ireland. Protestants have now gained a preponderating influence in the city (Montreal), but the whole country is peopled by French Papists. The English speaking inhabitants are comparatively few. Every village has its parish church, very much larger and more imposing then parish churches generally are either in Scotland or England. It should stir one's spirit within him to see a country so wholly given to idolatry. When I come home I shall be able to tell you more of Popery than I have ever known before. I count it idolatry as stupid and sinful and soul destroying as the idol worship of the Hindus. When Babylon falls, great will be the fall of it. Oh, for the brightness of His coming to destroy it!

Muir was quite unimpressed by Arnot, though the latter was probably the most gifted clergyman encountered by Muir during his tour. (William Arnot, *Autobiography of the Minister of the Free St Peter's, Glasgow and afterwards of the Free High Church, Edinburgh, and memoir, by his daughter, Mrs A. Fleming*, London, 1873; *Fasti Ecclesiae Scoticanae*; W. Ewing, ed., *Annals of the Free*

Church of Scotland, 1843–1900; T. Brown, *Annals of the Disruption*, new edn., Edinburgh, 1890; *Montreal Gazette*, 31 May, 14 July 1845; *Quebec Gazette*, September 1845).

55 The building in which Muir worshipped was burned down in 1856. 'The English church in Notre Dame Street, is one of the handsomest specimens of modern architecture in the province; it is spacious in its dimensions and elegant in its structure, and surmounted by a lofty spire, with timekeepers of the four faces of the belfry', J. Bouchette, *The British Dominions in North America* (London, 1832), i. 222.

56 James Nicol was about fifteen years older than his brother Peter. Prominent in Aberdeen affairs, James, in partnership with David Monro, was involved in shipbuilding in 1841. The following year they were importing timber in to Aberdeen from North America, and making arrangements for emigrants to sail to Quebec. (J.A. Henderson, ed., *History of the Society of Advocates in Aberdeen*, New Spalding Club, 1912).

57 *The Awful Disclosures of Maria Monk as exhibited in a Narrative of Her ... Residence of Five Years as a Novice and Two Years as a Black Nun in the Hotel Dieu Nunnery at Montreal* (New York, 1836). The work inflamed passions on both sides of the Atlantic and ran into several editions. Later various works appeared which refuted its allegations.

58 The designation, Mr Allan, advocate, fits three persons: George Allan, born 1820, who was admitted to Aberdeen's Society of Advocates in 1844; John Allan, admitted to the Society in 1841, and for a time in partnership with diarist Alexander Muir; Alexander Allan, admitted to the Society in 1810. The last named emigrated to Canada in 1843 and for approximately ten years was Superintendent of Schools in the Wellington District, Ontario. He died in 1855. Who, however, was the Mr Allan that Muir drank tea with? Was it perhaps the Superintendent of Schools on a visit to Montreal? Or even William Allan who died in Toronto in 1853?—a native of near Huntly, Aberdeenshire, who became a well-known Canadian businessman, financier, judge and politician. (J.A. Henderson, ed., *History of the Society of Advocates in Aberdeen*, New Spalding Club, 1912; *Dictionary of Canadian Biography*, vol. viii).

59 A canal at Lachine was mooted as early as the end of the seventeenth century. Work on the 'modern' canal commenced in 1821 and was completed four years later. R.M. Ballantyne, on his canoe journey, arrived at Lachine on 25 October 1845. He wrote

The village of Lachine is prettily situated on the banks of the St
Lawrence, about nine miles above Montreal. The country
around is populous and pretty, and the view across the river
beautiful. Just in front of the Hudson's Bay House—where I
was soon installed—is the Lachine Canal, up and down which
steamers and barges are constantly passing. Beyond this flows
the majestic river St Lawrence, here nearly two miles broad; and
on the opposite shore lies the village of Ookanawagan, inhabited
by a tribe of Iroquois Indians. Lachine itself is very small; its
only street, however, is well peopled, and the houses of which it
is composed are scattered over a large space of ground. The
Hudson's Bay House is the most imposing building about the
place, but it does not reflect much credit on its architect. There
are three churches in the village: a Presbyterian, Episcopalian
and Roman Catholic church, the latter being most generally
attended by the inhabitants, who are chiefly French-Canadians.

(Stephen Leacock, *Leacock's Montreal*, revised edn., Toronto,
1963; J. Bouchette, *The British Dominions in North America*;
R. M. Ballantyne, *Hudson's Bay, or Everyday Life in the Wilds of
North America*, 2nd edn., Edinburgh 1848, 265).

60   No street of this name was in existence around 1845. It has been
      suggested that Muir really might be referring to Hochelaga St.,
      a corrupt pronunciation of which, heard by him, has been
      transformed into an even more corrupt spelling.

61   George Auldjo younger had married in 1816 Helen, daughter
      of the Hon. John Richardson (1754–1831), a Portsoy man who
      became a leading Montreal merchant, financier and politician.
      George's uncle, Alexander, had married Eweretta Jane Rich-
      ardson in Fordyce, Banffshire, in 1804. Charlotte Richardson
      whose marriage is noted here was the youngest daughter of
      the Hon. John Richardson. She married the Rev. J. Ramsay
      (chaplain to the garrison at St Helens, formerly of the Glebe
      House, Templemore, Ireland) at Christ Church, Montreal.
      (Old Parish Register, parish of Portsoy, Banffshire; *Dictionary of
      Canadian Biography*, vols. vi, vii, and viii; *Quebec Gazette*, 26 May
      1837, 19 September 1845, *Montreal Gazette*, 18 September 1845).

62   The Misses Auldjo were presumably George Auldjo's other
      daughters, Elizabeth and Eweretta Jane.

63   This was in many ways a boom time for steamers. They had
      come out of their basic, experimental stage and were showing
      their usefulness on the St Lawrence and other North American
      waterways. They were now an accepted means of transporting
      goods; they transported thousands of emigrants upstream from

Quebec; they towed sailing vessels up and down stream between
Quebec and Montreal. They provided a new source of enjoy-
ment and pleasure to those who could afford the cost of a
pleasure trip. Possible destinations were the Chaudière on the
Ottawa, the mouth of the Saguenay, or Kamouraska. George
Auldjo was a passenger in the *North American* on a trip to Kamou-
raska in July 1843. Other steamers about this time were: the
David Ames; the *Charlevoix*; the *St Nicholas*, the *Lady Colborne*; the
Montreal; the *Lord Sydenham*; the *Queen*; and the *G. Buchanan* on
the Chats Lake. (*Quebec Gazette*, August and September 1842,
24 July 1843; 9 August 1843, 28 June 1844; *Montreal Gazette*, 7
August 1845; *Bytown Gazette*, 15 May 1845, 3 July 1845, and
April 1844).

64   The Irish-born Thomas Moore, 1779–1852, who visited British
     North America in 1804. Circumstances surrounding the com-
     position of the poem are recalled by Moore in his Journal, J.
     Russell, ed., *Memoirs, Journal, and Correspondence of Thomas Moore*,
     vii, London, 1856, under 14 August 1835.

65   The height of Mount Royal is nearer 750 feet rather than the
     550 given it by Muir. It is most likely that this is the 'mountain'
     which Muir and Mr Auldjo drove round on Wednesday, 17
     September.

66   The Aberdeen Market of this date was one of the town's latest
     architectural sights. It was prominently sited on the west side
     of the newly constructed Market Street, almost at its junction
     with Union Street, the architect being Archibald Simpson
     (1790–1847). The Montreal Market which Muir refers to is the
     Bonsecours Market, construction of which commenced in 1845.
     For many years Bonsecours Market was used for Public and
     municipal functions in Montreal. The building still stands. In
     reality the Aberdeen Market was marginally the larger of the
     two, but the facade of Bonsecours facing the street was much
     longer than Aberdeen's, and this has misled Muir. (R. Ander-
     son, *Aberdeen in Byegone Days*, Aberdeen, 1910; *Archibald Simpson,
     Architect of Aberdeen*, Aberdeen Civic Society, 1978; W.P. Perci-
     val, *The Lure of Montreal*, revised ed., Toronto, 1964; S. Leacock,
     Leacock's Montreal; E. Meldrum, *Aberdeen of Old*, Inverness,
     1986).

67   Information kindly supplied by Mrs Mabel Ringereide,
     however, established that Mrs McNabb was a lady who had
     travelled quite widely, but who, at the time of Muir's meeting
     her, had been settled in Bytown for some years and had played
     a role in the social life of its more 'elite' inhabitants. Her first

husband was Richard Fisher Fellowes of the Ceylon Regiment, by whom she had three daughters; her origins were in the English county of Kent, and her maiden name was Morson. Her second husband was a son of a major in the 91st Highlanders who later became an inspecting officer for recruiting and who, it has been claimed, was a kinsman of Sir Allan Napier MacNab. (Army Lists; M. Ringereide, *The Flourishing Tree*, Ottawa, 1977).

68   Inverurie is a small town about fifteen miles north west of Aberdeen. Baillie George Lyon, 1766–1837, vintner and inn-keeper, was a senior magistrate of Inverurie for a long period of years spanning the turn of the eighteenth and nineteenth centuries. Baillie George Lyon and his wife Elspet Philip had at least seven children, four of whom emigrated to Canada. A daughter and son, accompanied by a cousin, came out in the spring of 1829. The son, Robert (born 1813), had been a student for three sessions in the class of 1826–30 at King's College, Aberdeen. Thanks to the influence of his eldest brother, already well established in a military settlement, Robert became a law apprentice with Thomas M. Radenhurst, lawyer. Within four years he had made his small contribution to Canadian history, for he was the Robert Lyon who was allegedly the last person to be killed in a duel on Canadian soil, at Perth, in the then Bathurst District, on 13 June 1833.

Some three years after the duel Robert's older brother also came out to Canada. This was Robinson, who took up his father's occupation of inn-keeper. For a short time he was at Richmond, in the then Carleton County, but then moved to the Bytown area, where he kept the (Royal) Exchange Hotel. This burned down in 1854 and though Robinson suffered considerable loss, being uninsured, he managed to re-establish himself in his trade. He was the possessor of an unusual combination of talents, being an accomplished horseman and a skilful violin player. In the Caledonian Society's Hallowe'en Concert at Montreal in the year 1866 'R. Lyons' (sic) was declared the best violin player in a contest in which five competitors each had to play a reel, a strathspey and a Scottish air. Robinson, it is believed, died in the 1880s. The grandson of Baillie Lyon who married Mrs McNabb's daughter was George Byron Lyon. What Muir does not report is that the daughter was by the first marriage. Her name was Mary Matilda Ottley Fellowes. After the marriage she and her husband adopted the style Lyon Fellowes. George Byron Lyon Fellowes died during his term of office as Ottawa's mayor. His widow lived on until 1912. (Old Parish Register, parish of Inverurie, Aberdeenshire; *The Royal Burgh of Inverurie, an Historical Sketch, c.*1902; J. Davidson, *Inverurie and the Earldom of the Garioch*, 1878, 259, 393; J. Milne, *'Twixt Ury and Don and Round About*, Inverurie, 1947, 88–91; 'Historical Sketch of the County of Carleton, Ontario', in the *Historical Atlas* for that County; *Canadian Biographical Dictionary*; *St John's Anglican Cemetery, Richmond, Ontario*, Ottawa Branch, Ontario Genealogical Society, Publication 76/4; Ontario Archives, Toronto, MU-2367, Letters of 2 December 1828 and 2 June 1829, George Lyon to Thomas Radenhurst; The Hon Justice Riddell, *The Duel in Early Upper Canada*, in Hamilton, Ontario, Public Library Special Collections; E. Shortt, *The Memorable Duel at Perth*, Perth, Ontario, 1970; *Globe and Mail*, 2 November 1866; *Ottawa Daily Citizen*, 16, 18 March 1876; *Ottawa Evening Journal*, 26 December 1912).

69 Mrs McNabb's 'two brothers, students of medicine in Aberdeen' were to become well-known figures in Canadian medicine. Unfortunately, there is no record of Frederick Morson, born 1808, or of Alfred Morson, born 1810, having studied at either King's College or Marischal College, Aberdeen. It is most likely that they attended some of the private classes in medicine which were held in the city. (W. Canniff, *The Medical Profession in Upper Canada, 1783–1850*, Reprint Edition, The Hannah Institute for the History of Medicine; P.J. Anderson, ed., *Fasti Academiae Mariscallanae Aberdonensis, 1593–1860*, ii, New Spalding Club, 1898; P.J. Anderson, ed., *Officers and Graduates of the University and King's College, Aberdeen, 1495–1860*, New Spalding Club, 1893; P.J. Anderson, ed., *Roll of Alumni in Arts of the University and King's College of Aberdeen, 1596–1860*, Aberdeen, 1900).

70 Mrs Robertson was probably the daughter of William Wedderburn, mason, and his wife Margaret Black, and was baptised in 1788 in Aberdeen. She was married on 18 February 1808 to John Robertson, Esq., merchant in Aberdeen. (W.P. Lett, *Recollections of Old Bytown*, Ottawa, 1979, 69; A. Wedderburn, *The Wedderburn Book*, 1898, 479–80, quoting from Aberdeen Old Parish Registers, births and marriages).

71 A clue to the tracking down of the doctor came in a notice which appeared in the Bytown Gazette of 20 November 1845. It announced that William Morris, from Montreal, a tailor and clothier, had opened premises in Upper Bytown, 'formerly occupied by the late Dr Gellie, and lately by N.G. Robertson, Esquire, of Brittania, Wellington Street'. James Duncan Gellie

was the son of George Gellie, farmer, in the parish of Forglen, Banffshire. He spent two years of study at Marischal College, Aberdeen, in the class of 1823–7. He became a surgeon, recognised by the Royal College of Surgeons, England. When he was given recognition by that body 26 December 1828, he gave his residence as simply Demerara. It is possible that he was for a time acting as a doctor on sugar estates in that colony. His family was associated with the area once called British Guiana: James' (half?) brother, Andrew, was described as a planter in Demerara; in December, 1835, a relative was awarded approximately £35 by the Commissioners of Slavery Compensation. By early 1831 Dr Gellie was back in Aberdeenshire. At the end of the same year he was a surgeon in Ellon, Aberdeenshire, and he married there on or about 23 November, 1831. His wife, Jane Wedderburn, had a daughter, Jane Seymour, in Ellon in 1832, and another daughter was born in Bytown in 1836. Some six months later, on 22 December 1836, James Duncan Gellie made his will in Bytown. In addition to his wife he appointed George William Baker, of Bytown, William Thompson, of Nepean, and Alexander James Christie, of Bytown, as executors. Dr Gellie died on 3 January 1839 at Bytown. In the same month that Gellie married Jane Wedderburn, he admitted that he was the father, by Catharine Moir, Moss-side of Skelmuir, in the parish of Old Deer, of an illegitimate son. The child was baptised George Gellie and he grew up, married, lived and died in Scotland. His direct descendants are alive in Aberdeen today. (Ottawa Land Registry Office, Abstract Book 500, and Lot 9, Plan 3962, Instrument Nos. RO 966 (Land Sale, Samuel Stratford to James D. Gellie), RO 1507 (Mortgage from James D. Gellie to John G. McTavish), RO 4327 (Indenture of Release between Jane Macintosh and John Egan); *Bytown Gazette and Ottawa and Rideau Advertiser*, 20 November 1845; P.J. Anderson, ed., *Fasti Academiae Mariscallanae Aberdonensis, 1593–1860*, ii, New Spalding Club, 1898; Old Parish Registers, parishes of Ellon, Forglen, Old Deer, Rothiemay, Aberdeenshire and Banffshire; Scottish Record Office, Wills of Miss Mary Gellie and Mr George Gellie in SC2/40/13,f.272, and SC2/40/18,f.138 respectively; Archives of Ontario, Surrogate Court, RG 22/168, Box 1, 1841, Lanark County, Will of Dr Gellie, Probate, etc.; National Archives of Canada, Reel M-553, The Christie Letters, MG 25, 149, vol. 4, letter of 18 May 1835, from Elizabeth Wilson to her brother A.J. Christie, and the two following letters; National Archives of Canada, RG 5, B9, vol. 62, 546–7, Gellie to Lt. Col.

Rowan, and from the Hill Collection, MG 24, I8, vol. 19, 4710–11, 4716–17, 4725–6 (each from Gellie to Chairman of Board of Health, Bytown), and vol. 22, 5748–9, 5793–4, receipts signed by Gellie; Parliamentary papers, House of Lords, (23,II) 1837, 1837/8, British Guiana, 273, Sums of Money awarded by the Commissioners of Slavery Compensation; The Royal College of Surgeons, England, letter of 19 May 1987 to George A. MacKenzie).

72   Gellie's widow married James Macintosh at Bytown 6 October 1840. Macintosh, a member of the firm Macintosh and Keefer, Bytown, 'Wellington Street, four doors from the Post Office'. Macintosh 'was the first lawyer who came to Bytown to practise the profession and was a prominent one up to the time of his death in 1842'—aged 32. (National Archives of Canada, Bytown in the Forties with Glimpses of the Thirties, by an Old Resident (viz. George Pringle Drummond, 1839–1890), 13, 29, 30; *Bytown Gazette and Ottawa and Rideau Advertiser*, 26 September 1838, 13 March 1839, 8 October 1840, 1 September, 29 December 1842, 20 November 1845; *Quebec Gazette*, November/December 1845).

73   When Muir returned to it on 23 September to collect his luggage he named it as Dunning's Wharf. Members of Dunning families contributed considerably to the development of both Buckingham and Cumberland Townships. Families named Dunning owned land, lots 11 and 12 of the First Range, in Buckingham Township, and it has been traditionally accepted that a wharf was located there. The site of the wharf is now in the village of Masson, Quebec. (*Illustrated Historical Atlas of the Counties of Stormont, Dundas and Glengarry* , 1879, Prescott and Russell, supplement of the *Illustrated Atlas of the Dominion of Canada*, Toronto 1881; Letter of 28 June 1985 from M. Pierre-Louis Lapointe, Archiviste régional, Archives Nationales du Québec, Hull).

74   Alexander Finlay and Margaret Muir. See note 37 above.

75   Squire Cameron: In 1841 there was a John Cameron in Cumberland on Lot 15, Concession 1, Old Survey. (Land Registry Office, No. 50, Russell, Ontario).

76   Information arrived at Bytown on 27 June 1844 'of the total loss of the Church in Cumberland, by fire on Sabbath last. The fire was first discovered by some persons on the opposite side of the river, about two o'clock, but the manner in which it originated remains a profound mystery; as the people who had attended public worship there, had all left the place about an hour before, and there were no persons near when the fire broke

out, so that no information on the subject can be obtained'. In October of the same year the Rev George Bell made use of the *Bytown Gazette* 'gratefully to acknowledge the receipt of £10, being a donation from His Excellency the Governor to aid in rebuilding the Presbyterian Church, Cumberland, lately destroyed by fire'. (*Bytown Gazette and Ottawa and Rideau Advertiser*, 17 October 1844; *Quebec Gazette*, 1 July 1844).

77 George Bell, the son of William Bell, Presbyterian minister in Perth, Ontario. George served for approximately four years as minister in Cumberland Township, being ordained on 30 May 1844. He also had spiritual oversight of Buckingham, on the other side of the Ottawa River. (*Fasti Ecclesiae Scoticanae*, v; W. Gregg, *History of the Presbyterian Church in Canada*, Toronto, 1885; *Matriculation Albums of the University of Glasgow, 1728–1858*).

78 Archibald Petrie was a retired purser in the Royal Navy; he is later referred to as Captain Petrie, but that rank is not a naval one. He was born about 1790 and his first naval warrant was dated 17 December 1812. In a form which he completed for the Admiralty, 24 June 1835, Petrie stated that he had been in the Royal Navy for 25 years, and had served as (acting) purser afloat, three years in war and eight years in peace. In that year, (1835) at the age of forty-three, he professed himself able and willing to serve at sea if required. Although area of land possessed is not necessarily a yardstick of wealth Petrie could be classed as one of Cumberland's better off settlers. On 19 November 1835, he was nominated Justice of the Peace for Bathurst District, and the following year for the new District of Ottawa. In the Rebellion of 1837 the First Regiment of Russell Militia was formed under Captain Archibald Petrie, and he was appointed a major by the Adjutant General's Office, Montreal in 1846. He became Warden of the Ottawa District and was elected the member for Russell to the second Legislative Assembly (1844–7) of the Province of Canada. Later, in 1858, he was made President of the Russell County Agricultural Society. (*Navy List*; Land Registry Office No. 50, Russell, Ontario, Various instruments for the concessions specified, including wills, and concerning Findlay and Petrie in Cumberland and Clarence Townships; letter of 19 March 1986, from Senior Deputy Land Registrar, Russell, Ontario, to George A. MacKenzie; *Bathurst Courier*, 24 November 1846; J.O. Côté, ed., *Political Appointments and Elections in the Province of Canada, from 1841 to 1865*, second edn., Ottawa, 1866; National Archives of Canada, Audet Papers MG30, D 1, 768–771).

79 The precise location of this family has not been found, but it is thought that Muir's hosts were the couple James Golightly and his wife Mary, who possibly came from Haddingtonshire, Scotland, and their daughter, Agnes. They were to have a grand-daughter, Jane or Jennie Golightly. She was to marry Murray Russell, son of Robert Russell, who married Jane Muir Findlay, daughter of Alexander Findlay and his wife, Margaret Muir. The name Golightly has not been found in today's Cumberland: Russells and Findlays are still, however, in the area. (Ontario Census, 1861, Cumberland Township, Enumeration District No.2; Ontario Census, 1881, District No. 104 Russell, S/District C Cumberland Division No. 1; Dale's Cemetery Transcriptions, Cumberland Township; Information from the Misses E. and I. Russell, Ottawa).

80 The city of Aberdeen stands on the River Dee.

81 A loyal address from the townships of Lochaber and Buckingham to the earl of Dalhousie, dated 11 February 1828, has among its signatories Hiram Bigelow, Levi Bigelow and Laurence Bigelow. Joseph Bouchette's *The British Dominions in North America* (1832), i, 199, mentions Bigelow's mill. 'In the three townships of Lochaber, Buckingham, and Templeton, scattered settlements were formed within the last five or six years, and mills built in each of the townships. Of the latter Bowman's and Bigelow's mills, on the river Aux Lièvres, in the 4th range of Buckingham, are entitled to particular notice'. Unfortunately the censuses of 1842 and 1851 are not available for Buckingham, but in the 1861 census for the area five Big(e)low families are recorded. With only two exceptions all of these Big(e)lows were born in Lower Canada. The exceptions are Hiram Big(e)low and, presumably, his wife, Mary, aged seventy-four and seventy-nine respectively. Both of them were born in 'America'. It seems likely that it was this Hiram who led Muir on his tour of inspection of the mills. (Scottish Record Office, Dalhousie Muniments, GD45,I/3/534/10, used and quoted with permission; National Archives of Canada, Census of 1861, Buckingham Township, Ottawa County).

82 Two factors contributed largely to the growth and development of the site (in the north east corner of the old township of Nepean) which was to become Bytown: the opening up of the Upper Ottawa to lumbering, and the construction and completion of the Rideau Canal, which was officially opened in 1832. Five years previously the settlement had been given the name Bytown, after the Royal Engineers officer in charge of the

canal's construction, Lieutenant Colonel By. The name survived
a proposal, made in 1835, to rename it Aberdeen, in honour of
the then colonial secretary, the fourth earl of Aberdeen. But
Bytown it remained until 1 January 1855, when the name
Ottawa officially came into use. At the time of Muir's visit the
population was about 7,000. It still had features of a frontier
town. The population, a mixture of persons of Irish, Scottish,
English and French origin, did not always mix very well, and
in its early days the town had a reputation for lawlessness and
disorder. Notwithstanding this earlier reputation the town was
declared the capital city of Canada in 1858.

83   Alexander Christie was a son of Alexander James (best known
      as A.J.) Christie (1787–1843), a student at Marischal College,
      veteran (perhaps) of the Napoleonic wars, self-professed doctor
      of medicine. A.J. came to Canada, probably in 1817, and prac-
      tised as a doctor as well as founding the *Bytown Gazette* in 1836.
      The younger Alexander was probably born in Fyvie, Aber-
      deenshire, around 1813 (his grandfather was Episcopalian min-
      ister at Woodhead, Fyvie). He became a well known mason and
      builder in the Bytown area, and was immortalised by W.P. Lett
      for one of his achievements:

                .....that well remembered day—
                When the old town was wild and gay.
                From verdant vale to sunny ridge,
                On which the new Suspension Bridge
                Was opened—and crowds congregated
                To see it then 'inaugurated'.
                To use a word from Uncle Sam,
                The concourse was a perfect jam.
                'Twas built by Alexander Christie,
                From the land of mountains misty;
                And though the whirlwind and the storm
                For years have revelled on its form—
                Though ponderous loads for many a year
                Have passed it o'er from far and near,
                It stands in strength unshaken still,
                A monument of art and skill;
                Long may the builder dash the tide
                Of Jordan's swelling surge aside;
                And when the lot of all mankind
                Overtakes him, may he safely find
                A bridge across to Canaan's shore,
                To pass in peace death's valley o'er.

Sandy Christie 'passed death's valley o'er' in 1880. (W.P. Lett, *Recollections of Old Bytown* (Ottawa, 1979): published by permission of the Historical Society of Ottawa, the copyright holders). C.C.J. Bond, 'Alexander James Christie, Bytown Pioneer. His Life and Times', in *Ontario History*, lvi, 1964; P.J. Anderson, ed., *Fasti Academiae Mariscallanae Aberdonensis, 1593-1860*, ii, New Spalding Club, 1898).

84 James Christie, 1795–1837 graduated at Marischal College, Aberdeen, in 1812. He became a surgeon and resided at West Crichie in the parish of Old Deer, Aberdeenshire. (P.J. Anderson, ed., *Fasti Academiae Mariscallanae Aberdonensis, 1593–1860*, ii, New Spalding Club, 1898).

85 Susanna Watson Strachan was born 28 January 1819, at Anguston, Peterculter parish, Aberdeenshire, daughter of John and Ann Strachan, née Smith, who had died at Hull, Lower Canada 6 July 1836. John Strachan had been in Upper Anguston certainly between 1801 and 1823, latterly described as tenant and then as farmer. With his wife and some of his family he had left Aberdeenshire at a date unknown and settled in the Hull area of the Ottawa Valley. Susanna married Alexander Christie at Bytown on 15 January 1839. She died at Ottawa 6 February 1891. (Old Parish Register, parish of Peterculter, Aberdeenshire; *Bytown Gazette and Ottawa and Rideau Advertiser*, 16 January 1839; information from Dr Bruce S. Elliott, Ottawa, Ontario).

86 'Robertson' is an error; see account of 'Robinson' Lyon in note 68 above.

87 This may have been 'Chas Sheriff, sen., Esq. of Fitzroy', whose death at Bytown was announced in the *Bathurst Courier* of 25 May 1847. 'Mr Sheriff was an old resident on the Ottawa, and was highly esteemed by all who had the pleasure of his acquaintance'. 'Dr' Alexander J. Christie (see note 83) founded and owned the *Bytown Gazette*, and is usually regarded as being its editor in its early years.

88 Jamie Johnston was an auctioneer in Bytown. He sat in the second Parliament of the Legislative Assembly for the Province (the United Province of Lower Canada and Upper Canada).

89 Muir has written Clarendon for Carleton.

90 The Sheriff: presumably Edward Malloch.

91 Nicholas Sparks, 1792–1861, an Irish emigrant, timber merchant and landowner in the Bytown area. There is an article on him in the *Dictionary of Canadian Biography*.

92 The dwarf who so took up the attention of Muir and his friends,

was called Mr Nellis. He was part of a show which toured the Montreal-Bytown-Quebec triangle during September and October 1845. The *Quebec Gazette* acknowledged its debt to its rival *Mercury* for the account it gave of what the dwarf could do: 'Mr Nellis, born without arms, performs the most extraordinary feats. With his toes he writes, winds up a watch, loads and discharges a pistol, draws a bow, plays on the accordeon and triangle, cuts likenesses in paper and executes a variety of other astonishing performances'. This type of 'entertainment' was not uncommon at the time, and Muir may well have known of 'The Smallest Person in Creation', who was exhibited by Mr Laskey, at No 34, Broad St., Aberdeen at the end of December 1836. (*Aberdeen Herald*, 31 December 1836; *Montreal Gazette*, 26 September 1845; *Quebec Gazette*, 13 October 1845).

93 Not identified.

94 The district of Dalhousie comprised the townships of Fitzroy, Goulbourn, North Gower, Gloucester, Huntley, March, Marlborough, Nepean, Osgoode, and Tarbolton. The District was more a lumbering than an agricultural one. It is not to be confused with the Dalhousie Township in the Bathurst District. (W.H. Smith, *Smith's Canadian Gazetter*, Toronto, 1846).

95 William Thomson was a son of the John Thomson, a Scot who had settled on Lot 29, Concession 1, Ottawa Front, in the Township of Nepean. The Thomsons became well established in the area and built the fine residence of Maplelawn. They had considerable interests in lumbering, but were also progressive agriculturists. (M. Newton, *Maplelawn, The Thomson-Cole-Rochester House, 529 Richmond Road, Ottawa, a History, 1831–1979*, Ottawa, 1979; *Bytown Gazette and Ottawa and Rideau Advertiser*, 10 October 1844, 16 January, 24 July 1845; information from Dr Bruce S. Elliott, Ottawa).

96 George William Baker had been a Captain in the Royal Artillery and with his wife and family (including a son, George William younger) came out to Canada in 1832. By 1834 the elder G.W. Baker was postmaster at Bytown. By 1845 'G.W. Baker' was a magistrate in Nepean and the office of Postmaster at Bytown was still held by one of that name and initials, though it is not clear which was the father, which the son. (Army Lists; *Smith's Canadian Gazetteer*).

97 The fact that Muir had been a show judge did not take long to be published in his home area. The editor of the *Aberdeen Herald* wrote in the issue of 1 November 1844 'We see by the *Bytown Gazette*—a Canadian Paper—that our neighbour, Mr Muir of

Loirston, has been officiating as a judge at the Dalhousie District Agricultural Society'.

98   Gilbert Heron came out to Canada in 1834. Birness is in farming country in the parish of Logie Buchan, Aberdeenshire, about four miles north east of the small town of Ellon. Gilbert and his wife, Janet Sheppard, whom he married in 1813, and their family made their home in the Junction Gore of Gloucester Township. He was the founder of the Heron Settlement and his name is commemorated today in the main street name, Heron Road. (*Ottawa Citizen*, 10 September 1927; information from Dr Bruce S. Elliott, Ottawa).

99   Francis Smith has not been identified, but see note 101 below.

100   The Episcopal incumbent at Bytown during Alexander Muir's visit, whom he probably heard on Sunday, 5 October 1845, was the Rev. S. Spratt Strong. The church Muir worshipped in was demolished in 1872.

101   Is Muir speaking of someone not previously mentioned? Or is he referring to Mr Francis Smith, whom he met on 3 October, and has got the gentlemen's names mixed up? It is ironic to have this confusion on almost the only occasions on which he gave christian names to the persons he met!

102   Thomas Coltrin Keefer was to become one of Canada's foremost civil engineers. He died, honoured at home and abroad, at the ripe old age of ninety-four in 1915. For the most part taught in the hard school of experience, he was involved early in his career in work on the Erie and Welland Canals. When Muir met him he cannot have been long in his government post, which meant the oversight of roadworks, canals and timber-slides (particularly improvements to the two latter) in the Ottawa Valley. The *Bytown Gazette* of 3 July 1845 reported that

> We learn that Government are now directing their attention to the roads that are wanted along or near the river Ottawa, on the south side of the river above Bytown. Mr Keefer, an Engineer of the Board of Works, retuned to this place a day or two ago, from the Bonnchere, having inspected the road from Bytown to the Bonnchere, by Packenham and the White Lake, and, on his return, the road by Arnprior, Fitzroy Harbour, and from thence along the ninth concession of Fitzroy, to Huntley, March, etc. We hear that Mr K. will proceed immediately to make a further survey, for the purpose of ascertaining the most eligible line of road between Bytown and Pembroke, the highest surveyed township on the right bank of the river.

(*Royal Society of Canada, Proceedings and Transactions*, 1915, Obituary of Thomas Coltrin Keefer; Samuel and Thomas Keefer, 'Pioneers of Canadian Engineering', in *Engineering Journal*, 51, 1968, 14–18; Ontario Archives—M.W. Keefer, *George Keefer*, London, 1931).

103 James Blackburn (1799–1851) was the second son of Andrew Blackburn ('manufacturer' in Bridgeton, Glasgow) and Isabella Lennox. Financial problems led to the closure of the family firm of Robert and James Blackburn, Cotton Spinners and Power Loom manufacturers, creditors receiving their final dividend in 1830. Andrew Blackburn and two of his sons came to Canada and settled in the Hull area in 1829. His wife and another son followed in 1830, and James arrived in 1832. James Blackburn was a popular, respected person in his new homeland. He kept a store; he was a pioneer of steam navigation on the Ottawa (on the stretch of water up to the Chats); and for the years 1834 to 1838 he was a Member of the Provincial Assembly, representing the then County of Ottawa. He later removed to the state of Illinois, where he died of cholera in Bairdsville in 1851. James married Elizabeth Campbell in Glasgow Barony Parish on 5 April 1824. She was the sister of James Campbell, a founder of the firm of Glasgow warehousemen, J. and W. Campbell. He later purchased an estate in the county of Angus and became known as Sir James Campbell of Stracathro. His second son was Sir Henry Campbell-Bannerman, the Liberal Prime Minister of Great Britain, 1905–8. James Blackburn and his wife, Elizabeth, had five children born in Glasgow: Helen Forrester in 1826; Robert in 1827; Isabella Lennox in 1828; James in 1830; and Elizabeth Campbell in 1832. It is not known which of the girls was the 'very beautiful young woman' seen by Muir. (Old Parish Registers—Kilbarchan, (Renfrewshire), Glasgow, (Barony), Glasgow, (City); *Glasgow Herald*, 9 April 1824; *Glasgow Post Office Directories, 1820–1835*; *Biographical Sketches of the Lord Provosts of Glasgow*, Glasgow, 1883; *Burke's Landed Gentry, 1894* and *1914*; *The Edinburgh Gazette*, 26 June 1829, 30 July 1830; *Montreal Gazette*, 7 May 1845; *Bytown Gazette*, 12 September, 24 October 1844, 15 May 1845; National Archives of Canada, Audet Papers, MG 30 D 1, 717–725; information from Mrs Joan MacKay, Ottawa).

104 Various factors militate against the pinpointing today of this burial ground—the changes that have taken place in the Ottawa River over the last 145 years, the vagueness of Muir's description (one cannot say precisely how far or in which direction he

walked on the forenoon of 8 October to come across the burial ground), and the lack of death and burial records for the period. It may be that eventually the names Barnett Macdonald or Francis Bruneau will provide an important clue. In the meantime we can only speculate. Two possible sites have been suggested. The first is the cemetery of St James, part protestant, part catholic. The second is a field to the south of the Front Road (mentioned in J. Lloyd Armstrong, *Clarendon and Shawville*, Quebec, 27), where lay the cemetery associated with the old Chapel of St Alexander, which existed on Lot 24, Range 1, of Clarendon. (Letters to George A. MacKenzie from Mrs Venetia Crawford, of Campbell's Bay, P Q, 26 September 1985, and from Eric W. Morse, Wakefield, P Q, 25 March and 21 April 1985; Pierre-Louis Lapointe, Archiviste Régional, Hull, P Q).

105 This is Gerrard Nagle (1807–84), who was Overseer or Superintendent of Public Works. Gerrard was the eldest son of Garrett Nagle who, with his wife Honora and their family of six sons and one daughter, set sail from Cork, Ireland, on board the *Hebe* on 8 July 1823. Reasonably prosperous in their native County Cork, they came to Canada as 'Peter Robinson' settlers. The family settled originally in Ramsay Township, Bathurst District and were soon engaged in lumbering. Over the period of approximately fifteen years prior to Muir's trip the timber wealth of the Ottawa Valley was being exploited in an increasing measure. Smith's *Canadian Gazetteer* (Toronto, 1846), for example, says

> Great improvements have been made in the Ottawa in the last year or two; slides and dams have been constructed at various places to facilitate the passage of lumber down the river; and many obstructions in the course of the stream, such as rocks, etc., have been removed.

At the time Muir met him, Gerrard Nagle was engaged on this type of constructing. He had built for his family and himself a stone house (now no longer standing), on Grand Calumet Island.

Thomas Coltrin Keefer (see note 102) was the Engineer in Charge of the Ottawa Works and he reported to the Secretary of the Board of Works, late in September 1845 that he would 'employ Mr Nagle to complete the chaining of the line of road established between Bytown and Boucher' until he had received some instruction from the Board regarding Mr Nagle's position. On 15 October 1845 Keefer reported that 'I returned from the

Joachim last night. I am now engaged in arranging the details of the Slides, and Slide repairs and will in a special report on the Joachim, accompanied by a sketch, explain the damage and the repairs and alterations required'. (Public Archives of Canada, RG11, Vols. 6 and 7; *Quebec Gazette*, 31 May 1844; Private information from Nagle family descendants, Mrs M.N. Gallagher, Cambridge, Ont., and Mrs F. Kimpton, Windermere, B C).

106   Not to be confused with the better known Fort William on Lake Superior. An old French fort had previously stood here on the Ottawa, the Fort des Allumettes. It had belonged to the North West Company, but was taken over by the Hudson's Bay Company in 1821. The site was on the north bank of the Ottawa, just above the Allumette Island, in an area once much frequented by Algonquin Indians.

107   Hector McKenzie, born 1811 in the parish of Knockbain, Ross and Cromarty, son of Hector McKenzie and his wife, Ann Finlayson. He was related to the HBC traders Duncan and Nicol Finlayson. As Muir says McKenzie was 'from Inverness' he presumably lived there before emigrating to Canada. After his apprenticeship years as a clerk (1833–5), McKenzie spent some years at Fort Garry and Lower Fort Garry. In 1845 he came to the Ottawa River and was based at Fort Coulange and Fort des Allumettes in charge of the District. Most of the rest of his time with HBC he was based at Fort William. It is interesting that Muir should use the term Fort William as early as 1845. McKenzie retired in 1865, resided for a time at Gollanfield House, near Inverness, and died at St Leonard's on Sea in 1882. McKenzie married in 1849 Mary, the sister of the author R.M. Ballantyne. By her he had one daughter, Isobel, born 1852. Some ten years previously, when in the Red River District, he had had a relationship with a métis, Letitia Bird, by whom he had a daughter, Mary. (Sir George Simpson, *Narrative of a Journey Round the World*, London, 1847; W.S. Wallace, ed., *Documents relating to the North West Company*, Champlain Society, 1934; R.H. Fleming, ed., *Minutes of Council Northern Department 1821–31*, Champlain Society, 1940; M.A. MacLeod, ed., *Letters of Letitia Hargrave*, Champlain Society, 1944, particularly letter no. 29; E. Voorhis, *Historic Forts and Trading Posts of the French Regime and the English Fur Trading Companies*, Ottawa, 1930; J. L'Esperance, 'The Mystery of Miss McKenzie', *The Archivist*,—a bimonthly of the National Archives of Canada—1985; Summary of McKenzie's HBC service and of Fort William dates

provided by HBC archives, Provincial Archives of Manitoba, Winnipeg; Royal Ontario Museum, Toronto).

108 *Joachins*: should be Joachims. A notice dated Kingston, 27 April 1844, authenticated by D. Daly, Secretary, dealing with various slides, appeared in the *Quebec Gazette* of 13 May 1844: 'The Provincial Slides at the Deux Joachims, the Calumet, and the Mountain, on the River Ottawa and at the High Falls, on the River Madawaska, are now on the eve of completion'. Rates of tolls for the passing of timber were given. In his report to the Secretary of the Board of Works, dated 8 November 1845, Thomas Keefer gave details of what had happened at the Joachims.

> The slide is much injured from the effects of high water and loose timber and had it not been relieved by the loss of the entrance pier it must have been swept off. The slide has settled in the grade; the posts forming the sides are sprung from the perpendicular, the planking of the bottom and sides in many instances carried away—the south head pier gone—the north entrance pier, through which the great body of water flows, also gone, and one of the loop piers damaged.

(National Archives of Canada, RG11, vol. 6, 1756–59).

109 Thomas Keefer had five half-brothers and four full brothers. (A.D. Fordyce, *Family Record of the Name of Dingwall-Fordyce in Aberdeenshire*, Fergus, Ontario, 1888).

110 The earliest notice which has been found of the Rev. George Tulloch as a teacher in Aberdeen or its immediate neighbourhood is from the spring of 1834. In January 1835 he announced that he would soon be ready to receive boarders at Bellevue. The curriculum was a broad one, but the basics such as reading and writing were not neglected. Specialist instruction was to be provided by visiting masters. A method 'so successfully pursued by the late Professor Jardine in the Logic Class of the Glasgow University' was to be employed in the educating of young gentlemen of above fourteen. French was taught, and indeed was the language of conversation in the family (Mrs Tulloch was born in Calais). Mr Tulloch advertised his Academy as a select school, his own role in it not being underestimated—'evening studies and *even* amusements will be conducted under his own superintendence'. Terms for board, lodging and education were £40 per annum for young gentlemen under ten; forty-five guineas for young gentlemen between ten to fourteen years; and fifty guineas for those over

fourteen. Each pupil had a 'separate bed', but had to provide two pairs of sheets and six towels. Fees had to be paid one quarter in advance and three months prior notice of leaving was required. Washing and other extras were paid for separately. The school was situated between present-day Dee Street and Crown Street in Aberdeen, in the street which today bears a clear reminder of it—Academy Street. Indeed the building is still (1988) in existence, externally much the same as in Tulloch's day; internally it has been altered for use as a meeting-place by religious denominations, mainly Baptist and Plymouth Brethren. George Tulloch appears to have been responsible for running Bellevue Academy until his death in 1873. It therefore became something of an 'institution' in the city and indeed was also known as Doctor Tulloch's Academy.

The boarders were accommodated at Tulloch's residence, Bellevue House, in the Hardgate. Pupils such as George Muir therefore had a walk of about one and a half miles to reach the Academy. Tulloch's enterprise seems to have met with success— at least round about the period of which we write. In 1841 there were fourteen boy boarders between the ages of nine and fifteen, plus six student boarders between fourteen and eighteen. Of these boarders four were born in Canada, four in India, one in each of New Brunswick, Buenos Aires and France, and two in Ireland. Three female servants were employed. In 1851 the roll of Boarders had increased to thirty-five boys, the youngest aged eight, the eldest sixteen. There were now four female servants, plus a cook. But no increase had taken place in the number of resident teaching staff—still at three: Mr Tulloch, of course; his cousin, Marcus Tulloch, MA, who taught for more than thirty years at the Academy; and John Falconer, who had been, by 1851, replaced by John Fiddes, MA.

George Tulloch had been baptised at Wick, Caithness, on 15 August 1797, the son of John Tulloch and his wife, Barbara Henderson. He may well have received his early years of education from his father, who was also a teacher. His period of study at King's College, University of Aberdeen, was a broken one: his first year was in the class of 1814–15, but he did not graduate until 1830. Yet in the year previous he had been asked by his Alma Mater to deliver his first Murray Lecture—'On the Parables of Our Lord'. And he was so honoured again in 1830 and 1834. King's College conferred a Doctorate of Laws on him in 1847. The date and place of his licensing as a minister have not been traced, nor his induction to any charge. 'This well known citizen and estimable man' died in Aberdeen on 29 April 1873. He was buried in St Machar's Cathedral, Aberdeen and a commemorative tablet was placed there by his former pupils and friends. (*Aberdeen Journal*, 30 April 1834, 7 January 1835, 7 May 1873; *Aberdeen Directories*, 1830–77; P.J. Anderson, ed., *Officers and Graduates of the University and King's College, Aberdeen 1495–1860*, New Spalding Club, 1893; P.J. Anderson, ed., *Roll of Alumni in Arts of the University and King's College of Aberdeen 1596–1860*, Aberdeen 1900, 78–9, 118, 285; A.M.Munro, ed., *Records of Old Aberdeen*, ii, New Spalding Club, 1909; Census 1841 and 1851, City of Aberdeen Old Machar Parish).

APPENDIX 1

Letter from Alexander Muir to Alexander Findlay, 11 September 1845

The following letter from Muir to his brother-in-law provides some information, additional to that contained in Muir's diary, about his intentions after the point at which the diary ends. It also indicates that Muir's brother, George, had recently visited Scotland. The 'Pegg' mentioned is presumably Margaret, Muir's sister. The original is in private hands.

Haste

Mr Alexander Findlay,
      Cumberland District,
Care of Captain Pettrie
      by Bytown
      U.C.   Quebec, 11 Sept. 1845

My Dear Brother
    I arrived here on Monday night, and intend to leave this evening for Montreal. I am to remain over Sunday there and will start for your place on Monday. I understand it is [at] McLeod's Wharf I leave the boat on the Ottawa River, but this will reach you in time I hope to drop me a few lines at Montreal for my direction—as to what way I will get my luggage over to your place. I have brought a featherbed and some blankets so don't give yourself any trouble with me.
    I have heard nothing of my brother's family and Dr Stewart since they left Aberdeen, but we met the *Heroine*, the ship they went out on, on her homeward passage. I intend to remain with you for two or three weeks until I see all your part of the country properly, and then

I go up to George and home through the States by New York—but I fear this will now be next spring.

As I am in haste to get underway I shall conclude by wishing I may find Pegg and all well.

yours faithfully,
Alex Muir

you may address
>Mr Alex Muir,
>>from Aberdeen
>To be left at the Post Office till
>called for,
>>Montreal

APPENDIX 2

Account of a Voyage from Aberdeen to Quebec by William Shand, 1834

William Shand emigrated to Canada in 1834, and the following account of his voyage is contained in a letter to his brother-in-law, Alexander Ragg, in Dufftown, Banffshire. Shand travelled on the *Hercules*, and the 'Mr Wal^r' mentioned was the commander of that ship, Captain Walker. The original spelling has been retained. The account is reproduced by kind permission of Mr and Mrs J.R. Shand, Port Dover, Ontario, Canada.

My Dear Sir

I make no dubt but the recept of this will give you all some satisfaction to know that I am safe landed on the Coast of America which I did in good health and also all the rest on at Quebic.

There is but little that I can give in the way of newes or information as we have had but little time to colect them, and I would not have time to write much if I had.

Along with this I have sent you a kind of a scrol of our Passage and some Newes Papers—which I hop you will receve, for altho the Jurnal be a jumble of every thing as it hapned without any kind of order or regulation yet they may enable you to form some Idea of the comferts of a sea voage also of what is to be seen by the way—which I dar say you will not much admire how ever we could a been much worse. How ever we had reason to be thankful for we could a been much worse & I belive upon the whole it is but rare to be so well—and what contributed a good deal to that was the attention of our Capt. It is but Justes to Mr Wal^r to say that in my opinion there is not a man better adapted for his busness than he is—a very clever shrewd man with a great deal of experence and so completly sober that he teasts no drink of *any kind* stronger than wa^r and seems to have his thoughts upon nothing but his busness and the comfort of his crew—

113

he acted as Surgeon to the whole of them when the were sick, wisiting them each day giving them meadeson—wines etc. [?] all gratuos (he has a meadson [medicine] chest & directory). Should it hapen that I continue in this country, when my folks comes out I should above any thing wish that they were under his charge and am certain that he would pay every attention as if they were his own and I would have an easey mind on there acc[t]. With respect to my self I had not one hours sea sickness all the way—but I was seased with a kind of leasenes—that I hated to do any thing—even to read or write and a lothing to every thing either of meat or drink, for the first 4 weeks and there scearce was any thing that I could teast but Brachan and Bros[1] for a considerable time tea, and Coffee, was out of the question—for to my perverted teasts the sea water it self would a been much more pleasant and above every thin thirst was the worst—the water that we had the first 4 weeks being in cours [coarse] mollashes casks became so bad in a short time that it was impossable to disgese the teast of it with any thing whatever—and, I was many times that I would a gladly given a s/- for one Bottle of good small Beer. To be at sea a gain I would have a Dozen or 3 of Small Beer in fine [?] to any other thing for I have been often that I would a gladly given a shilling for one bottle however before we landed I had com prety well round— the thing that was worst for me was the fall with the stair which brused my right side so much that I had great pain to lay in bed for 2 or 3 weeks. I had also near two days of my old complint the head ack very veoilent.

We had 7[2] of Steerage passangers in whole several of them was whole familys: farmers, and others and some single men who had left there familys and treads from the diferant parts of Banff, Aberdeen and Mearns Shire and 5 from Katness [?]—there was 25 children under 12 years—this with all the different grads and characters colected made up a gay noasie [?] and had you been placed on a trunk in the corner or laying looking out of the Bed to them as I have been at all the different motions that that was going on you would a been a good deal amoused—but to give some Idea—sepose [?] 5 or 6 next you playing cards with as many on the oposate side playing Dams a little farther on 2 or 3 smoking and debating on the ships progress and how far we had yet to sail (and I shall not say that these statements would a been allways corect), then other 2 or 3 singing songs with some pairs here and there of the different sects carrying on something in the way of courtship—then round the fire (which is nearly in the center) 6 or 8 of the wives some with there children squaling others fighting who should have on her pot first—with pos- ably a fiddler playing on Dack to a number dancing over you with such a noise that you would think they would send the dack down on you and the stars and hatch between dacks of in gress & egress I could compare to nothing that I think it is so like as to the door of a strong Bee Hive in a fine summer day whene there would be allways a number going out with as many coming in: all this with coursing and swearing and speaking Galiec, composed something like the sight and sound of the Group.

In the Cabin was a Mr Clerk with his wife and seven children—he is a Brother of Tallachalams first wife—he had a fine Farm near Coulan [Cullen?] on which he fealed [failed] his a Brother in Londan [London], a Dr Clark who it seems wished him to go to America is giveing him asistance—and he had also furnished him with a great many of the latest publications on Amer.—all of which he gave me one by one to read & which was amusement to me for a considerable time—he is a Joviall kind of fellow with regard to my prospects here I can say nothing yet but I shall not feal to communicate to you from time to time every occurance which shall happen—and I hop *you* will nether be sparing in your paper nor ink to me as there is nothing that will give such pleasure as to hear frequently of all your wellfare and prosidings—tell Mrs Ragg that if I shall see any prospect of a settlement in this country where I could think to place my family any ways comfortable that I shall not despair of seeing you all there also—and as she had use to say that she was afraid for crossing the sea—tell her that can be no hindrance as it is only Ideal and by no means real—for altho very few of our crew had ever been at sea before I do not sepose that there was one on Board that by the time we was 24 hours out entertained more fear than she dos in her own Bed Closet—and in reality there is no danger more at sea than land—for if clear of Coast and Rocks and a good ship, accidents is as near as to a house falling or taking fire and burning and if it was not for the expence and loss of time I would think no of more of crossing to an from America, than of going from Dufftown to Aberdeen on the Mailcoach—for altho I was A little squeamish with it at first it was greatly owing to my Ignorance of not knowing how to behave—and guide myself— and you can tell Baby that no thing that we had that added more to comfort, than the chaff Bed, and that I slept softer all the time than I had in her feather bed in the closet.

I hop you are prety well acquant with what is dowing about the Kirktown and that the little folks there is well—tell Elspet and W^m that if they forget any of there catchisims or pa^r that I shall not send them any thing from America—but that if you can inform me they have advanced well in there reading and writing and got a good many more of the ps—& parph^s—there Cath^s—and behave well that I will try to send them something with the fall ships— tell Baby that I expect to hear how she is getting on with her Cows and Sows.

Tell Ann that I will be most excedenly disapointed if she does not behave herself to the satisfaction of Mr and Mrs F who has proved so singular friends to me and if you see any of them make offer of my very warmest gratitude and best wishes and hope to hear when you write that they are well—give my good wishes to all enquiring friends and all the old neighbours round the Kirktown espesely Helen and El⁵ Gʳ.

I hope if you have not wrote as you receive this that you will do it instantly as I will be in the greatest anixety to hear from you—you can direct it to lay at the post office at York—and how soon I know whos care I could have letters directed I shall inform you

1   Brachan or brochan is a gruel or porridge; brose is a dish of oatmeal with boiling milk or water.
2   Probably seven *parties* of passengers is meant.

APPENDIX 3

Account of a voyage from Aberdeen to Quebec by William Fasken, 1837

William Fasken and Alexander Muir were near enough to being exact contemporaries and both had their roots in the soil of Aberdeenshire. William Fasken was born, it is believed, in the parish of Forgue in 1782. He became a stone-mason and worked on the building of the Bell Rock Lighthouse. Then he and his wife, Margaret Mitchell, after a residence of twenty-two years in Forgue, decided to emigrate to British North America. Eleven Faskens were among the thirty-one passengers who sailed from Aberdeen on 30 May 1837, on board the regular trader *Quebec Packet*, 196 tons, Captain W. Stephen. She was operated by the Aberdeen firm of Robert Catto and Son. She arrived in Quebec on 22 July, her crossing taking longer than average. According to Fasken family tradition William was engaged for a year or two in the construction of military fortifications in the Canadas. Afterwards, he and his family travelled westwards in Ontario and settled on Lot 1, Concession 7, of Nichol Township, an area which welcomed a great number of early settlers from the North East of Scotland. Lot 1 remained in Fasken ownership until just after the end of World War II.

Neither Fasken's spelling, which has been preserved, nor his writing can match Muir's, and a few of his words remain undecipherable. It must be said that it cannot have been easy to keep a diary while sailing steerage. The original is in the Fasken Family Collection in the Archival Collections of the University Library of Guelph.

(Sources: Aberdeen Harbour Board Records, Sailings; *Aberdeen Herald*, 3 and 17 June 1837; *Quebec Gazette*, 24 July 1837; D.M. Beattie, *Pillars and Patches, a History of Nichol Township*, Ontario, 1984; Information from Mrs Doris Wardlow, Missouri).

1837, May 30, Sailed from Aberdeen, 9 o'cl. pm.
2 June, sailed into Longhope.

4 June, Sailed from Longhope.

6 June, last sight of land.

16 June, First ship in sight, at a distance.

17 & 18, Very stormy weather the Ship hove too for 30 hours.

28 June *Phenix* of Grenock in Long 44.40 homeward bound. She was alongside. Could not Speke. Rough Weather

29 June, Spoke a Barque belongin to Plymouth: the weather More Mild. From the 17 to 29 June the Weather was Extremly cold.

1 July, a great calm and we hade a cod fishing.
   Spoke the *Crison*[?] of Sunderland, From Quebec, in Long 53.40.

5 July, bloed hard and a heavy sea. Cape Rea, the first land, in sight about 10 miles distant at sunset.

7 July, Near the [-?--?-] Captain shot 14[?] Solan goose.

12 July the mouth of the River St Law. Anticostie on the North and the Coast[?] of New Brunswick on the South.

16 July, 200 miles below Quebec. Past the *Roaiy* [*Royal*] *William* of --rand, her daks crouden with passengers. From the 18 June to this date with little exception we hade Westerly Winds: this day saw the first human habitation Except the lighthous at Anticostug. Near when [sic]. Near the midle of the river could see the land on both sids Near this shore ar Roky and Mountainous.

INDEX

The following abbreviations are used in the index:
Co. (County); N.B. (New Brunswick); N.S. (Nova Scotia); Ont. (Ontario); P.E.I. (Prince Edward Island); P.Q. (Province of Quebec); Twp (Township).

119